C·H·A·N·G·E·S

John Michael Talbot

C·H·A·N·G·E·S
A Spiritual Journal

❋

CROSSROAD · NEW YORK

1984
The Crossroad Publishing Company
370 Lexington Avenue, New York, N.Y. 10017

Library of Congress Cataloging in Publication Data
Talbot, John Michael.
Changes: a spiritual journal.
1. Talbot, John Michael.   2. Composers—United
States—Biography.   3. Fransciscans—United States—
Biography.   I. Title.
ML410.T139A3   783.6'092'4   [B]   84–15567
ISBN 0–8245–0665–0 (pbk.)

C·H·A·N·G·E·S

Preface

It is Wednesday—the one day a week that I must leave our peaceful Franciscan hermitage in the mountains and trek the twelve miles to our community offices in town. So here I sit behind my cluttered desk, staring at the unusual array of articles on and around it: an open Bible close at hand, icons of Jesus and Francis on the walls, an in-and-outgoing mail bin that never ceases to overflow, and the modern office phone complete with a Watts line that competes for attention with an ancient gas room heater. All of these material things symbolize the spiritual paradoxes, creative tensions, and healthy changes in my life as a "modern Franciscan hermit." They indicate that all my life in Christ has been, is, and will continue to be a life filled with healthy changes.

The following pages are excerpts from my personal journals. They were written at a time of great upheaval and change in my own life, and therefore reveal my deepest questions and doubts, and my endeavor to find authentic answers in faith. Most were written at Alverna House of Prayer in Indianapolis where I was led to put the pieces of my life back together after a painful divorce. Others were written in motels, monasteries, and airports, from Florida to California to Canada. But it was at Alverna that I began to pray for guidance from the Lord about my vocation in life. At that time I was recognized as a professional musician of

1

some celebrity and as a "Jesus freak" of some notoriety; at Alverna, I began to realize that Jesus doesn't make freaks out of people; he makes people out of freaks. And soon my music, my message, my ministry, my entire way of life began paradoxically to soften and grow stronger, grow gentler and take on new assurance, turn inward and reach out for community.

Sometimes, to my surprise, these entries seem to reveal mature thought, while at other times they manifest the primitive seeds of what flowered into maturity later. At still other times they clearly show how humorous our "serious" questions can be when viewed from a comfortable perspective of a few years' hindsight. These thoughts are thus not intended to be a theological treatise nor a systematic devotional aid. They simply reflect many of the internal questions and struggles I faced during a time of great vocational decision in my life. I lay the pages open and the thoughts naked before the reader, both in gratitude for the direction God has freely given me, and in the hope that God may choose to use even a single line to be of comfort or help to others on a similar journey.

All of us face our times of struggle and decision in Christ. Few of us are called to follow Jesus as a Franciscan or as a hermit; yet all of us must face the challenge to take up our cross and follow Jesus Christ without compromise. This implies change—change that is sometimes painful, yet a change that leads to the health of a new life in Christ. It is my prayer that this open sharing of my own personal journey will help you in yours. It is my prayer that we all find Jesus as our rock of salvation in the midst of the challenges of living the gospel in a constantly changing world.

So I resume contemplating my icons, reading my Bible, and answering my phone. I know that throughout my whole life, God will call me to devote some time to each. I must pray, I must meditate, and I must minister to others. And I know that these ministrations will all flow in and out of one another in the rhythm of the Spirit, just as the mountains around our hermitage change with the rhythm of the seasons.

But enough of this rambling; the phone will soon be ringing and

I shall probably be buzzed by my secretary to *talk* to someone about contemplative silence. Praise God for his grace and that tomorrow is Thursday!

Your little brother in Jesus,
John Michael Talbot

Eureka Springs, Arkansas

March–April 1978—
Alverna Retreat Center, Indianapolis

Five visions of vocation were given to me by the grace of Jesus over a seven-year period, beginning in 1971 and continuing until the present year of 1978. Perhaps more perceptions and insights are yet to come—perhaps not. But ever since my wife's remarriage, I've felt a growing confusion and have recently given my changing vocation in Jesus a great deal of thought.

These five visions seem to sum up the new vocation Jesus is calling me to, for they have been planted deep in my heart, and I can't stop thinking and writing about them.

The first vision was a vivid picture of an agrarian community of prayer. The second concerned an apostolate of poverty. The third emerged during my divorce and took the form of a stong sense of assurance through scripture about that apostolate of poverty. The fourth was a clear call from Jesus to enter the Catholic Church. And the fifth vision was of an old and tattered habit. An examination of these personal revelations may shed light on the vocation to which Jesus is calling me.

The first vision came one night during prayer, and it was as if Jesus were painting a beautiful picture of a Christian community right before my eyes. It was the most harmonious painting I have ever beheld, for it was filled with love and peace. Selfless love and unity characterized every aspect of this community of Jesus' followers, both in their dealings with one another and with nature. In this vision all of creation was reconciled to the way of Jesus; his followers not only spoke of his way, they also lived it.

The Spirit of Jesus filled each member of this contemplative community. Jesus and the ethic of his cross were living personally in each of their lives. The same Jesus who taught and lived out love for mankind as no man had done before, who walked the face of this earth two thousand years ago in humility, poverty, meekness

4

and gentleness, who died so that all mankind could live . . . this same Jesus was resurrected in their hearts so that *his* love and *his* life could continue through *their* lives. Every moment and every action became a sacred and spiritual event in which Jesus graced their being by his presence through his Holy Spirit. This community knew true contemplative peace, for they knew the living presence of Jesus that stirred up in their hearts a continual attitude of solitude, silence, and worship.

Because the love of Jesus continued his life through their lives, all the members of this community shared all things in common. Each member gladly embraced the *poverty* of Jesus so that others could embrace the *wealth* of Jesus. Each gave so that others could receive. Consequently, all basic needs were met in the community, and the living love of Jesus was manifested there so that all the world could see that "he is risen."

The love of Jesus also blessed the community's relationship with nature. In supplying the basic needs of food, clothing, shelter, and energy, the well-being of nature was always protected by looking to God's guiding truth as revealed in scripture and in nature itself. The way of the cross was always followed in trying to reconcile a creation raped by man back to the tender love of Jesus.

The community members themselves produced most of the food they shared. They were tillers of the soil and keepers of the garden. They kept lovely fields, orchards, and vineyards, using hand tools and small machinery. They worked hard but stayed healthy with a combination of exercise and plenty of natural food. They gathered and hunted in the forests that they were careful to preserve between agricultural fields. They kept flocks and herds of domestic animals, which they watched with care and compassion so as not to take the joy of life from them. In this way, the community followed God's original ordination for man: to till and keep the sacred garden.

Their clothing was humble, simple, and practical; made from natural sources, it became the outer sign and reminder of an inner spirit of poverty. They did not dress vainly to impress others. They simply dressed to cover nakedness, both for the sake of protection

5

from heat and cold and for the sake of avoiding any stumbling into lust. Styles were tailored for flexibility in circumstance, but fairly uniform so as not to give occasion to pride. In all, the clothing produced by the community manifested the way of Jesus' humility and poverty in every stitch.

Shelter was also simple and practical, the style of architecture lending itself to an efficient use of material, space, and energy, as well as to purpose. Most homes were made of rock, wood and earth, and I presume were mostly underground, for I could see only small rounded enclosures aboveground serving as an entrance.

Energy sources were used in harmony with the way of the cross concerning man's kinship with nature. Most sources were non-polluting and easily replenishable, thus insuring a long-lived relationship of balance and harmony between man and nature. Energy was used mainly for cooking, heating, and some lighting, since energy sources were needed for little else in life.

The entertainment for the community could be described by one all-inclusive word, *worship*. Seeing the experience of the cross living in all things, community members became as dead men so that Jesus could live. Thus in all things the Creator of all life graced them with a marvelous gratitude for life. Dead men are indeed thankful for *new* life! These Christians could live every waking moment in wonder and thanksgiving for their new life in Jesus, seeing that they had all died with Jesus in their Baptism. It was through this attitude of continual worship that everday occurrences and jobs were tranformed into miraculous wonders of life. So in a worship that included contemplative private prayer, the liturgy, recreation, and the physical work of the community, each member was entertained beyond imagination. Worship was the *life* of this contemplative community.

It was this first vision that urged me to a contemplative community of prayer, a community of peaceful unity and harmony, a community of everlasting love. Jesus has called me to this kind of community and only he can now make it a reality in my life, for the love of Jesus and the way of his cross is this community's source of life. Jesus has led me to the first step in realizing my life's vocation in him.

The second vision, again given during prayer, called me to an apostolate of poverty among the churches of Jesus. I saw myself clothed in a brown, coarse garment resembling a habit and walking on foot from church to church to share the simple love of Jesus. The *message* of the apostolate was not the important call of this vision, but rather the *mode* of the apostolate was. In this vision Jesus called me to a ministry that did not depend on anything other than two legs and a voice to bring his message to the world. Being free from huge expenses, this apostolate could thus be offered to the world as a gift of grace, just as Jesus offered his apostolate to the world as a gift of grace. Only poverty brings the freedom to bring the wealth of Jesus without charge.

In the third revelation, Jesus assured me through scripture that although I would lose my home, my wife, my child, and my property, he would grant me the wealth of the kingdom, the family of the saints, and the home of my spiritual mansion if I would undertake this apostolate of faith and poverty to share his love with the world. To this day I still seek to accomplish this in a better way. It is the core of the gospel message, and to it I can only respond, "so be it."

The fourth vision came at a time when I was seeking a unified Christian church for a new spiritual home. I sought—and found—a church that could ensure the way of the cross and the way of unity based on the love of Jesus through that which he had ordained. In this vision Jesus called me to enter into the Roman Catholic Church, a church I used to attack verbally. He simply said, "This is my ordained church. She has been sick near death, but I am raising her to new life through my Spirit."

I was to find in this church the remnant of mystical devotion to the cross of our Lord Jesus existing without compromise. I would discover an ordained, governmental structure capable of housing our spiritual unity in Jesus. Certainly, I still saw fallibility and gross error in her history, for she is made up of imperfect men and women. But I also saw in her the potential for an indelible and sometimes infallible spiritual structural unity that could manifest the way of the cross to our world. Through study I learned that this unity of Spirit and structure based on the love of Jesus has been infallibly promised to the church by Jesus himself, and it can come to pass only in an apostolic structure ordained by Jesus. I found the Catholic Church to be that structure.

The fifth perception came at a time when I was considering the similarity between my call to an agrarian prayer community and an active apostolate of poverty within certain of the religious orders already existing in the church of Jesus. I saw a striking similarity of spirit and action between the visions of St. Francis of Assisi, St. John of the Cross, St. Benedict, and Thomas à Kempis and my own vocational call from Jesus. Granted, many of these orders no longer resemble the visions of the men whose names they bear, but most continue at least in charity, which is the greatest gift, and some are still faithful to their original visions.

So it was at this time that the fifth vision came calling me to the religious life. An angel simply came during night prayers and extended that familiar old, tattered, and torn religious habit to me. It did not resemble the many habits often worn today simply for pious show. This habit was to be worn by one too poor to have anything better to wear. It was to be worn as an outer sign of an inner and practical condition—of spiritual and physical poverty. It was a call to the cross of Jesus. To this day I have yet to respond totally, but the day will come when I will say, "so be it."

It is to these vocational calls by Jesus that I now seek to respond. I seek a Christian community that manifests the way of the cross in all areas of life; a Catholic-oriented community of prayer and worship; a community of selfless love in dealing socially with one another and the world; a community that reveres nature and follows God's ordination in taking what it needs from her; a community that allows each person the solitude to be with Jesus; a community of communication that allows each person the silence to hear the word of Jesus in his heart; a community of stability that

8

is a home to its members, yet is balanced enough to allow them to follow Jesus in his apostolic mission to the world; a community of poverty that offers the wealth of a life in the Spirit of Jesus; a community of mystical death that offers eternal life in Jesus, the giver of life.

I seek this community within the context of existing community structure. I understand the idealistic nature of my call, but I also realize that patience and obedience can make the vision and call more realistic in practical application. I feel I should learn from and be willing to submit to an existing structure before God will allow my vocation to be uniquely realized. I seek to temper my idealism with practical application, and to strength my future by learning from the wisdom of the past.

The question is this: Are there any religious communities with similar visions, and if there are, am I an acceptable prospective applicant for membership?

June 7, 1978—11:30 P.M.—Alverna

I am thinking again about my vocational call to a contemplative agrarian community and to an apostolate of poverty. Since there were women and children in the community vision, and since I was also given a vision of the garment of poverty, yet aware of my own lack of community experience and the sparsity of apostolic missionary work in most contemplative agrarian communities, I am led to wonder if there may be different stages in my vocational call.

It seems likely that I could first spend some years of preparation in a contemplative agrarian community before embarking on my vocation to an apostolate of poverty, and before helping others to establish similar communities for lay people. It makes much sense to learn from the wisdom of the past before trying to shape the future. Therefore, spending time in a religious community that

9

emphasizes contemplation in solitary and communal prayer, the study of religion, philosophy, and the arts, and manual labor in the agrarian vein would be almost mandatory if I am to help others to establish well-rounded lay communities. In fact, my vision of the religious "habit of poverty" makes this very likely. But only God can show me the way for sure, and I am grateful for his promise of guiding us to truth by his Spirit.

June 8, 1978—8:30 A.M.*—Alverna*

When the time comes for me to embrace both an active apostolate of poverty and a contemplative life of silence, prayer, and manual labor, it seems that the contemplative life should be emphasized. A cup must be full before others can drink from it without drinking it dry, and a contemplative prayer life of solitude and silence fills the cup of our life.

A good physician treats both the symptoms and the cause when trying to heal the sick. Likewise, in our sick world-system the community of contemplative prayer manifests Jesus' healing of the cause of sickness, while an active apostolate deals only with symptoms. Both are necessary, for the pain and agony of a disease's symptoms are cruel, and only a person devoid of Jesus' compassion and love could ignore those who suffer from the effects; but it is always more important to deal with the cause of an illness if we truly seek total healing for today's world. So if I could exercise my calling to an apostolate of poverty in harmony with my calling to community of contemplative prayer, I would have to emphasize the contemplative calling. Only then would I be able truly to manifest the healing of Jesus to a sick and pain-burdened world. Only then could I offer the living water of Jesus' Spirit to a world parched and dry that even now begs for something of substance to drink.

10

June 8, 1978—10:00 A.M.—Alverna

It seems good to emphasize that these communities of contemplative and agrarian life-style can be monastic for religious orders and secular for lay people. Jesus outpours his Holy Spirit on both the celibate and the married, and creation waits to be released into the glorious liberty of *all* the sons of God. The celibate and married states equally manifest the love of Jesus and the ethic of his cross, which reconciles all of creation back to the harmony of God. In my first vision of an agrarian community of contemplation and prayer, I saw both women and children living normal, happy lives. Their joy rested in the fact that Jesus and the ethic of his cross had become a living reality in their lives and their community. So, potentially, an agrarian Christian community of contemplative prayer can fill the cup and heal the cause of the disease in both the religious and the lay life in Christ.

Vocationally, this means that while I am called to a celibate life in a contemplative religious community, my apostolate of poverty may act as a catalyst to inspire and help lay people to establish similar communities. Such an apostolate could come only from living experience, so I would assume that this would come at a later point in my religious life. But I must assume the responsibility of the vision that includes both religious and lay Christians in an agrarian, contemplative community.

June 8, 1978—1:00 P.M.—Alverna

A contemplative community has exciting possibilities in the areas of study and manual labor, as they relate to my personal call to vocation. Because of my present apostolate of preaching and teaching, it would be good to study theology and philosophy along with their historical impact on culture. Because of the gift Jesus gave me in music, it would also be good to study both classical and liturgical music so as to nourish worship in my private and public apostolate. Because of my interest in the Christian community's impact on ecology, it would be good to study various aspects of nature, gardening, and alternative energy sources. The latter would also encompass my involvement in productive manual labor. Obviously, both study and manual labor would be carried out in an attitude of contemplative prayer so that they may be truly fruitful.

Again I must always remember the contemplative aspect of these studies. An inner attitude of prayer and worship must never be hindered by active study. It is undertaken only to glorify the Lord and help nurture an attitude of responsible and disciplined stewardship in the community member. Even in preparation for a possible apostolate, contemplative study and prayer are necessary to arm the warrior for spiritual warfare. So an attitude of solitude, silence, and prayer must be present if either study or labor is to be fruitful.

June 8, 1978—3:00 P.M.*—Alverna*

Above all else, I seek only to embrace the cross of Jesus. He calls me to this more than anything else. I am called to his death so that I might know his resurrection. That is my all-important vocation.

The weakness of the cross is the strength of our mysticism. The humility of the cross is the exaltation of contemplative prayer and worship. In the solitude of the cross is our true communion with Jesus. In its childlike simplicity is the ancient wisdom of ages that is the object of our study. In its gentle silence is the bold proclamation of the love of Jesus. The constant giving of the cross is the true receiving of the gift of Jesus. Its emptiness is the fullness of giving to the needy. Its thirst is the never-ending well of living water given to the thirsty. Its final cry to the Father is the source of forgiveness that imparts the gift of inner silence to the world.

So the cross is my contemplation and my apostolate. Only in silence may I speak; yet only in speaking will the world hear the word of beautiful silence. All is paradox; yet all is true. All is mystical dread; yet all is peace. May we never go beyond the paradoxical cross of Jesus, for if we do we will have surely gone too far and lost the truth of Jesus. In this will I find true contemplative peace. In this will I find my true apostolate.

So come Lord Jesus, let me embrace your cross.

June 9, 1978—8:00 A.M.*—Alverna*

On this bright and beautiful morning the life of Francis seems very close. He was a contemplative hermit; yet he was also an apostolic preacher who could live in community with his brothers and preach to laymen by word and action. In this he followed the example of Jesus who is the ultimate example for all Christians.

In his rule, Francis leaves room for the contemplative life in community or in the hermitage. He also takes it for granted that there will be preaching and works of charity directed to the layman. Francis never ceases to emphasize the contemplative life of silence, solitude, and prayer, but he also never excludes the life of apostolic preaching and charity when carried out in the contemplative spirit. Both Francis's life and his rule capture the balance between the two that makes one truly free. He was truly an imitator of Jesus.

I recall an experience of spirit that occurred at the Trappist monastery of Our Lady of Gethsemani in Kentucky. While walking in the wooded foothills, I felt filled with the Spirit of Jesus. I sang to the birds and the flowers and they sang to their Lord. Even the rocks of the earth sang to their Lord Jesus. Just then I was aware of the presence of three people over and above me. These people were Jesus, Mary, and Francis!

I felt a vocational call to the monastic stability and silence of the

Trappist, the freedom and complete devotion of Francis, the humility and obedience of Mary, and most of all the forgiving love of the cross of Jesus. So in this experience I can see the totality of my vocational call from Jesus.

I pray that Jesus gives me the strength to respond and the wisdom to know what the practical application of his call might be.

June 10, 1978—10:40 A.M.— *Tampa Airport*

I would like to make note of my present feelings concerning my active apostolate in the ministry of music.

I first embarked on this apostolate three and one-half years ago as a response to a call from the Lord. He told me to speak to issues, to urge the lazy and the self-righteous to repent and reform, to prepare a yet spotted and ugly Bride for the coming of her Groom by admonishing her to good works, forgiveness, and a love that would make her beautiful to behold. He told me the degree of acceptance and popularity he would give me. He gave me the songs to sing, the albums to record, and the concerts in which to appear. So, after three and one-half years, two albums, and hundreds upon hundreds of personal appearances, I look back and see that my apostolate has fulfilled the early vision God gave to me.

But lately, since my entry into the Catholic Church and the fulfillment of my apostolic ministry, I have sensed a change in myself. Instead of resembling the bold and brash Elijah or John the Baptist, I have begun to resemble the soft-spoken and gentle Francis of Assisi. In this weakness, I am finding a new strength and power. In this humility, I have found the ministry of the cross of Jesus. In a sense, I moved from the way of the old covenant to the way of the new covenant in Jesus. So, for a time, the weakness and gentleness of my apostolic ministry has soared beyond expectation in power and authority.

Even more recently, I have sensed my previous ministry of song and exhortation coming to an end. It is as if I am riding into shore on a wave that originated in a strong tempest at sea. As I embrace the cross ever more to my heart, I am amazed to sense the disappointment of my audience. This disappointment is not a spiritual disappointment. It is a physical disappointment. They came to hear powerful attacks on a hypocritical church, and I tell them to *forgive* the church and submit to her as a structure ordained by God. They came to hear powerful oratory, and I meekly tell them of silence. They came to hear deep theological explanations and to find black-and-white answers in "the Word," but I tell them of a simple relationship with the living Word, Jesus. Oh, I am not saying they disagree with what I share, but I do not tell them anything they really don't already know. Sometimes I feel they are disappointed with this message of the cross after having driven several hours, and having waited in a long line, expecting to hear something the world would consider "powerful." The cross is power, but it is weakness in the eyes of a world to which even Christians are so accustomed to conform. I wonder whether the message of the cross's simplicity is enough to dazzle the audiences of my music ministry, but dazzling, I now know, is no longer "enough."

June 10, 1978 — 11:30 A.M. — Tampa

I think it goes even deeper. God ordained me to my past apostolate of calling people to repentance, and graced it with effectiveness and fulfillment. But while Jesus has personally drawn me closer to his cross, I have yet to feel an anointing by the Spirit to carry this message exclusively in an apostolate. It is as if Jesus allowed it in this time of change; as if its success and acceptance were a carry-over from my previous apostolate until I could clearly hear his new call; as if it did not yet really stand on its own, but was dependent upon something that had come before. But now my previous apostolate is gone. It is a memory, not reality, and even difficult to recall. So while I do not question the validity of apostolates by men who embrace the cross, I must seriously question whether or not God has at this time called *me* to such an apostolate. Perhaps this weakness is not entirely "worldly," but is also a weakness of spirit from a lack of true anointing and ordination by Jesus.

June 10, 1978—12:00 Noon

More and more Jesus is calling me to a contemplative life, drawing me yet nearer to the cross of his solitude. In silence, I come into a true companionship with Jesus and truly converse with the living Word. I feel the call to the desert, so that I may appreciate his living water. I seek simply to disappear, so that I might be found. Yet I feel this living Word of silence too profound for me to belittle with a multitude of words. I feel it communicated only by a few short words or perhaps only a smile or a countenance, for this profound silence can be truly communicated only by the Holy Spirit. I now question whether those touched by my ministry would be satisfied with such a doctrine or such a "performance." They are simply too accustomed to an American Christianity of constant talking, constant action, and an abundance of stage tricks guaranteed to keep their attention when the weak silence of the cross no longer "dazzles." But it is not their fault, since they have been fed little else.

With the disappearance of my previous apostolate, I now feel free to respond personally to the call of Jesus. I am free to follow him into the desert or to the mountaintops, to commune in solitude and silence with the Father. In this silence, I will hear the word of Jesus and sing praises with my heart. In losing my life, I will truly find it. This is a strong call I now hear from Jesus.

Practically speaking, this means a life of prayer, study, and manual work. I cannot speak of silent prayer without harming it, yet silent prayer is the most important part of this life. Regarding study, I feel the Lord would have me learn more of theology, philosophy, history, liturgy, classical music, and nature. I have informal knowledge in many of these areas, but it would be good to understand the wisdom of the past more fully in order to help shape the future. The manual work would involve putting into practice my knowledge of liturgy and music, and also I would love to become involved in gardening and alternative energy sources once again. I still have much to learn in all these areas. Of course, all study must be transcended by an attitude of contemplative prayer and praise to the Lord our God.

At the present time, I feel Jesus calling me to a contemplative life that emphasizes solitude, while still retaining some community life. Even hermits, who speak seldom, are a working community by their unspoken support of one another. I desire community if it be possible, for "it is not good that man should be alone," but I also realize that it is only in personal solitude that I can find the companionship of Jesus. Neither the hermitage nor the community frighten me; in fact I feel called to both.

June 10, 1978—12:30 P.M.— *Tampa Airport*

While my present apostolate now draws to an end, I see more clearly a valid apostolate in the hermitage or in the contemplative community.

First, there is that incredible apostolate of prayer. The contemplative, above all, should realize the power of prayer, for that is the source of his entire life. In solitude he finds the Companion who never leaves him alone . . . through prayer. In silence he finds the continual guidance of the living Word . . . through prayer. In losing himself he finds his identity in the self of Jesus . . .

17

through prayer. Prayer is the foundation of the life of the contemplative.

But Christian prayer, as an apostolate, finds its object in others. Thus is the contemplative truly conformed to the image of Jesus on the cross. In prayer we must know solitude only so that others may come to know the companionship of Jesus. We must listen to silence so that others may hear the voice of God. We must enter the desert so that others may drink of living waters. We must spend our nights in watching and prayers so that others may rest soundly in the loving arms of Jesus. In short, we must continually die to our own desires, so that in interceding for the needs of others, *they* may find life. In this loss of our own life, the contemplative finds an eternal life in *praying always* for the lives of others.

By the very existence of the contemplative hermitage or community, the apostolic ministry reaches fulfillment. Ideally, those hermitages or communities existentially manifest the heavenly kingdom on earth. In their solitude they have gone beyond the need for an outer companionship that causes one only to hide from the inner companionship of Jesus. In their silence they have gone beyond the constant speaking of outer words that serve only as barriers to keep us from hearing the simple word of God in the inner self. In their study they have manifested the search for God's truth in all things that surely guides this world. In their labor they have manifested the way of the cross that surely reconciles this raped creation back to the tender and gentle love-making of God.

Now it is not necessary for each individual of this community to have a preaching apostolate, music apostolate, or any public apostolate for validation. Rather, each individual has a valid apostolate simply by being part of the community and serving the community with the love of Jesus. By simply living the contemplative life, each individual, even the hermit, encourages the other community members to live the contemplative life of Jesus. Their prayer, their study and their labor cannot help but encourage others— even in the midst of solitude and silence. Just by living the contemplative life, an apostolate to fellow community members is fulfilled.

This simple "city of God" set on the hill of this world cannot be hidden. Through the simple course of life, people cannot help but come into contact with the contemplative community. Even in a substantially self-supportive community, some supplies must still be obtained by purchase or donation, and the surplus of the community's produce will undoubtedly be sold or donated to others. This involves normal contact with "the world." In time, many people are bound to become curious about this beautiful "city of God" and will come to ask, "Who built it?" Then the contemplative can simply and quietly say, "Jesus did." So in the silence and solitude of the contemplative life, one still speaks to others about the true companion of the inner man of us all, Jesus Christ. The city set on a hill cannot be hidden.

June 10, 1978—2:00 P.M.— *Orlando Airport*

A limited or guided apostolate of poverty in preaching and teaching is surely in line with the contemplative life, both are truly part of the gospel. We are told to go to the highways and hedges and invite the needy to the feast of Jesus. We are told to tell the nations. We are told that only in our speaking (not "talking") will they hear. Isn't it in keeping with the paradox of the cross that it requires words to tell people of contemplative silence? Didn't Jesus himself speak? A contemplative life that is truly patterned after Jesus Christ must have the freedom to allow those called by Jesus to an active apostolate to follow his call. Should we be so inflexible as to force an exceptional man called by Jesus to an active apostolate to obey man rather than God? Who could dare to tell God what his will is, when we speak his will as contrary to the gospel life of Jesus?

Now I am not saying that every man or woman called to contemplative life who feels like running off to preach in an apostolate

19

should do so. His call should be carefully and lovingly explored with his director or superior to determine its authenticity, and he should obediently submit to such guidance as unto the Lord. Even Paul submitted to the apostles in Jerusalem regarding his own apostolate. But the person who has an obvious call to an apostolate as well as to the contemplative life should be allowed to follow his call as long as his contemplative life is strong and sure enough to transcend his apostolate. This judgment should be left to God alone who would manifest his judgment through the individual's superiors and directors. So while the stable life of the hermit or the contemplative should be emphasized and guarded at all costs, the truly Christian community will leave freedom for the contemplative to embark on a guided and limited apostolate when Jesus truly calls.

Above all, we must follow the call of Jesus. If called to a contemplative community of hermits ... *follow*. If called to a contemplative community of cenobites ... *follow*. If called to an active apostolate ... *follow*. And if you are called to a combination of the three ... you must still *follow*! It is up to our religious communities to house those with various calls. I pray that we are open enough to structure our communities in such a way as to be a home for those truly called by Jesus. There must be "room at the inn" for every gift and calling.

June 10, 1978—4:00 P.M.— *Jacksonville Beach—Howard Johnson's*

So be it. In the near future, I see for myself the definite possibility of contemplative life in a community of men living in solitude and silence. I see it as normal for me if the community is truly a manifestation of the loving kingdom of Jesus. As I am drawn closer into the living reality of the cross, I find that both solitude and silence are the sources of my companionship and conversations with Jesus. I am not opposed to normal community life with other people, for I love them even as Jesus loves them when his Spirit is present with me in my inner solitude. But I see a life of substantial outer solitude and silence as the true norm of the kingdom of charity and love, for silence and solitude insure an even deeper companionship and communication with other people and with God. I am not afraid of a contemplative community of God's children living in solitude and silence if love and charity are its motivating force.

In fact, I consider such a community as the ideal norm for the realized kingdom of Jesus, for it is out of charity and love for both God and man that we enter into solitude and silence. In such holy quiet, man finds companionship and communication with Jesus without interruption. When Jesus lives in a man or woman of solitude and silence, that person will actively enter into community only to communicate the pure love of Jesus with others. So in allowing each man his solitude and silence, the community as a whole will be free of empty visits and one-way talks, and will come to know both men and God only through the companionship and communication of Jesus. Consequently, love and charity will permeate the community, for Jesus is love and charity.

I do not see solitude and silence as abnormal, but as the true and healthy norms for the spiritual man. I do not see them as cruel, though they can be frightening. I see them as the only way truly to hear Jesus' kind voice and feel his loving presence without interruption. It is frightening only when you don't find Jesus inside you; then you enter into the despair of loneliness and the agony of silence. But when Jesus lives within you, your solitude and your silence are sources for a deeper companionship and communication with his love.

Nor do I see this as a contradiction to the call of all believers to an apostolate. Our prayer is an apostolate. The life of community itself is an apostolate. The community's normal dealing with the world is an apostolate. So even if I were never again to embark on a public apostolate, I would see the contemplative community of

solitude and silence as a fulfillment of the normal call to an apostolate for all Christians.

I seek, however, a contemplative community that is dedicated
enough to Jesus and his gospel to allow the few men that are *truly*
called to an active apostolate to follow freely the Lord's call. They
should be able to do this without having simultaneously to deny
his call for them to live most of their life in a stable community of
solitude and contemplation.

While I seek the solitude and the silence of a community of
Christian hermits in response to his call, I do not seek to put God
into a box by excluding the possibilities of any further call. In light
of the vision of the apostolate of poverty among the churches, it
seems likely that I shall someday embark on an apostolate in a
manner very similar to the early monastic hermits or the early
Franciscans, who shared their gift with all the world. But in the
end, I seek only a life of contemplative solitude, silence, and poverty, in which there is no contradiction between a balanced life of
contemplation and apostolic action.

June 11, 1978—1:00 A.M.—
Jacksonville Beach—Howard Johnson's

I must also consider a completely different alternative,
namely that an apostolate of poverty would come first, and a new
contemplative order would grow out of that apostolate. It is possible that after the release of my next album (a contemporary Mass),
a fresh anointing will come upon my Franciscan apostolate of
music. Perhaps this present transition period is only waiting for
that to occur.

If that is the case, I would sell everything I owned except my
guitar and a few devotional books. I would clothe myself in the
tattered habit of the vision. I would set out on foot from church to
church, relying only on the grace of Jesus for support. I would sing

my songs of Jesus as a troubadour for the Lord for whomever would listen. In my weakness, my ministry would become truly strong, and my vision of a contemplative lay community would sprout forth from my apostolate.

I guess the only way to know is to submit my vision both of the contemplative life and of the apostolate of poverty to the church. In her structure, Jesus will give me an answer. If any religious orders accept my application and my vision as it stands, then I know that my vision for the future can fit into the existing structures of the present and the past. But if my vision does not fit any existing order of contemplatives, I will know that God has called me to bring forth something new for this present age. Just as Francis simply did not fit into the religious Orders of his day, so perhaps I do not fit into the ones existing today. Only in submitting the vision to the authority of the church can I know the will of Jesus concerning my next step.

June 12, 1978—6:00 A.M.*—Alverna*

Concerning my call to gospel poverty in my apostolate a few things need to be clarified:

My call to poverty is simply a call to the cross. The wealth of Jesus is in becoming poor so that another might know of true wealth. I must give all I have to those who have nothing before I can truly receive my gift.

My treasure must be only in heaven, so that my heart will be only in heaven. I must not be bound to defending an earthly kingdom and thus turn from the nonresisting example of our Lord and his cross. My heart is only on my heavenly treasure, and I am bound only to defend my heavenly wealth if I walk this earth in a poverty that seeks only another's wealth. My call to poverty is simply a call to the wealth of *Jesus* and the example of his cross, where he became poor so that the world could receive his wealth.

Being bound to pay the price of poverty is my source of true freedom if I am to give the wealth of the kingdom as a gift. The more material goods my apostolate depends on, the more I must defend and pay for. The more I need, the more my concert hosts are bound to ask for money from my audience to pay my expenses. Thus, my apostolate to share the gift of music I receive from Jesus would be changed into an apostolate that has to be hired out for a price. Whereas, in relying on little, I can ask for little. In asking for little, my sponsors can easily meet the need from their local church, and the apostolate can be offered to the world as a gift. Then, being bound to a poverty that asks for little, I am free to know the wealth of Jesus by giving much.

So if I possess only clothing, a guitar, and a few devotional books, I will be *free* to travel the world on foot, by car, or by plane to share the wealth of Jesus who prepares my mansion in heaven.

My call to gospel poverty as it affects my call to agrarian Christian community has, however, a more complex application, though it is still simply a call to the cross. The Christian community that would manifest a complete alternative or healing to the world-system must deal with both symptoms and causes. Therefore, it cannot depend upon the alms from the diseased world-system, lest the world see no viable alternative or truly workable healing in its existence. This community must rely on very little by living a life of relative poverty, and it must meet the true physical needs of the spiritual being in a way that is in harmony with creation. These needs are for food, clothing, shelter, energy, and entertainment. Therefore, the community needs land, livestock, and some basic machinery to produce these "products," which in turn will manifest the complete healing of Jesus and his cross to the world. So the gospel poverty of the Christian community will be very real relative to the standards of the average American, but it will not be the same as the poverty of the apostolate of teaching and music.

The Christian community that manifests only partial healing deals with only some of the symptoms, but it still needs support. It deals with the spiritual cause of disease by proclaiming the good news, but it can deal with only a portion of the physical causes for the diseases that now plague this world. It needs alms to support its activity in medical work, feeding the hungry, housing the homeless, providing jobs for the jobless, etc., and so ideally should beg alms only from a source that is free of disease, lest the diseased community see no true alternative.

Even the community involved in a more traditional apostolate of physical charity needs some possessions with which to minister to the world. They too will live in relative poverty compared to the standards in America, but will not live the poverty of those involved in an apostolate needing less material goods or finances to bring charity to the world.

We have two types of Christian communities in which my call to poverty fits. One deals with physical *causes*, while the other deals with physical *symptoms*. Both deal with spiritual causes, for both manifest the love and charity of Jesus that caused him to offer healing to the world. Both types of communities are valid and truly Christian. And both require physical things in order to exist. Therefore, the physical poverty of these communities will be less evident than it will in the few men involved in a teaching or preaching apostolate.

It would be good to consider the poverty of the contemplative prayer community. This community transcends the above-mentioned communities in its physical make-up. It is the most important of all communities, and ideally, every community should be first and foremost contemplative. But like the other two, it also requires material assistance. Even the hermit needs food, clothing, shelter, energy, and entertainment. Even the hermit will at some time produce something physical to aid the needy and the suffering. Even the community that considers itself purely contemplative will live a life that requires physical assistance or support. So they too will live in only relative poverty and, as a community, cannot come to the potential gospel poverty of the apostolate of teaching and preaching.

The individual in these communities, however, is still called to a strict life of poverty. He is called to possess nothing. All he uses must lovingly be held in common with his brothers and sisters in Jesus, for we are all one body. We cannot truly possess anything when we are all part of one another. What I have belongs to Jesus, and my brothers and sisters *are* his body on earth. What I have belongs to my brothers and sisters. I can truly own nothing.

While the overall community can continue to exist by living only a relatively poor life, the individual must be truly poor in spirit and body. He must never claim anything as his own and must respect the possessions of others. He must seek only to give, but must fight so that others receive their just payment. He must consider himself without rights, but must always seek to preserve the rights of others. In short, he must consider himself dead, but must always fight for the right to life all men possess. This is the cross of Jesus. This is poverty of spirit.

While the community as a whole still requires some possessions in order to exist, it must likewise manifest the gospel poverty of Jesus as a whole if it is to be truly Christian. While it may legally own possessions, it must consider itself only a steward of these physical things, used only to manifest the way of the cross of Jesus. The community must take only what it needs for basic survival and the continuance of its apostolate. The rest should be given to the poor. The community will thus fulfill its responsibility to guard over the physical and spiritual well-being of its members, while at the same time it will reach out to the world and other communities with the charity of Jesus. By binding itself to the poverty of Jesus, the Christian community will truly experience the freedom that comes with the wealth of Jesus.

June 12, 1978—1:00 P.M.*—Alverna*

It would be good to mention here that the poverty of Jesus does not condemn the wealth of others. We must never make pov-

26

erty a legalistic demand on all Christians. Our poverty has its object and fulfillment in another's wealth. This is the way of the cross. All Christians have the right to private property, but we have the privilege to hold all things in common. We have the right to wealth, but we have the privilege to become poor. It is only when you draw into the depths of the cross that you feel the call willingly to give up your rights to defend the rights of others. Let us who are called to poverty never judge or condemn the wealthy man. Let us defend his wealth in our poverty. Then will we freely grow into the way of the cross by the love of Jesus. We must never force a man to the cross, lest we grieve the Spirit of the cross and our Lord of love. Our poverty must have as its object the wealth and happiness of others.

The safeguarding of the contemplative life is another reason for my apostolate being carried forth in humble poverty. Jesus tells us that where our treasure is, there also will be our heart. He tells us never to be anxious for anything. He also tells us never to praise our own accomplishments, but always to let another man's lips praise us. If my apostolate is dependent upon a large cash flow or a huge advertising campaign, then it would be difficult truly to obey his word. I would soon find myself, and others in my ministry, worrying about the future cash flow as we dream up new campaigns to tell the public of my "great qualities"—so they will be sure to come and see me. Of course, this would all be done in the name of Jesus and his charity, but in the end my contemplative life would degenerate as humility turned to pride and my heart, once fixed only on Jesus, slowly turned toward material "necessities." Then I would have nothing of any real spiritual worth to share with the large crowds in an apostolate that might be materially worth a large sum of money. No one can serve both God and money, and pride surely goes before the fall. The contemplative life must be guarded in order that the apostolate be truly of God. An apostolate of simple poverty and meek humility is the only course I see that will not in time destroy the contemplative life.

History has shown us the downfall of contemplative life many times. The original contemplative community of the kingdom always prospered with an emphasis on growth of the inner man and his prayer of silence and solitude. This life produced spiritual men and women who had the fullness of Jesus' Spirit to share with the world. In the charity of Jesus, an apostolate was undertaken by only a few of these people, making sure the contemplative life was guarded and emphasized. The apostolates were patterned after the admonition of the gospel. They were simple, poor, and humble. In fact, this was what attracted the people. The extraordinary life of the missionary was in itself all the advertisement needed. Under the humility and simple poverty of such a life, the missionaries remained truly contemplatives, for their humbled hearts were fixed only on heavenly treasures.

But when the apostolate became too large and too dependent upon material wealth, the contemplative life always began to suffer. Hearts once fixed solely on heaven turned back to the world which became the weeds that inevitably choked out the true crop of contemplation (firmly planted in the garden of the kingdom). Soon, in the activity and worry of such an apostolate, the weeds grew and suceeded in choking out the true contemplative life.

The successful religious contemplative communities are usually the ones that have excluded the apostolate of preaching altogether. Because of the corruption of pride and materialism that always seems to creep in, most contemplative orders have totally excluded any active apostolate whatsoever. It is very hard to argue with this exclusion when one sees the spiritual happiness and the purity of the contemplative life of these communities compared to the lack of spirituality in some active apostolic communities that bear the name "contemplative" (both past and present).

Still, I get the feeling that these communities which exclude all apostolates have thrown the baby out with the bathwater. The baby Jesus is an innocent child who is very naturally both contemplative and active. Neither is excluded for neither is corrupted. The contemplative life of prayer and continual praise is emphasized, but the charitable apostolate is not neglected—when carried forth in the poverty and humility that guard the contemplative life! Pride and materialism have often spoiled the Body of the Christchild, but a bathing in the Spirit through repentance and prayer will always clean his Body. When throwing out the bathwater, we must be careful not to throw out the complete Body of contemplative love that the Christchild is.

We must hence take the chance of allowing the apostolate of poverty and humility. We must be willing to get a little dirty so that the world can be washed clean. Chances are that the dirt of pride and materialism will once more stain the pure contemplative Body of Christ. But when this happens, we have to believe that Jesus will simply place us back into his waters as he has done so many times before. If we never took a bath through repentance and prayer in his Spirit, then we would indeed have a problem. But Jesus has promised that he will keep his Body clean through washing us with his Spirit. We must be willing to become dirty to wash the world clean if we truly want to experience the washing of Jesus in our communities.

It is because of the above that I believe my personal apostolate should be one of poverty and humility. Relying only on food, some clothing, and my voice, I can walk the way of the gospel which insures that my heart be fixed only on heavenly treasure. Being humbly content to play for small gatherings, I will not be forced pridefully to "blow my own horn" to get people to come hear me. I will walk in poverty and humility, thus insuring that my apostolate be carried forth in the attitude of contemplative prayer in Jesus.

June 12, 1978—9:30 P.M.—Alverna

I am thinking tonight about chastity unto the Lord. Jesus and I have died together on the cross as lovers. Jesus and I have been resurrected from the tomb as lovers. In this new life, Jesus and I have been forever married. We have loved in the bed of our spiritual union through the cross, and he has impregnated my spiritual womb by the seed of his Spirit through the resurrection. I have grown full with the fruit of his Spirit as I wait to bring forth many children bearing his name. When he returns to me, I will present him with his children and we will celebrate the marriage supper of our union. So to deny my Husband would be to deny the life within me and the new life that will come forth from me—and I can do neither. So for me to be chaste unto the Lord is only this simple—he is my Lover forever!

It should be mentioned that chastity unto the Lord is manifested in the vows of both marriage and celibacy. Both are signs of our marriage to Jesus our Lover.

June 13, 1978—8:00 A.M.*—Alverna*

In the experience of the cross, I have become a dead man. Dead men cannot make decisions. It is only through the experience of the resurrection of Jesus that I have direction and new life. Therefore, any decision made in this new life must be made in holy obedience to the word Jesus speaks to me. It is the word of truth, the word of love, the word of new life. It would be foolish for a dead man not to obey this beautiful word of God that brings true life.

Jesus is the example we use for obedience. He submitted to the will of the Father in all things, and recognized the authority of the Father in the authority of men. Jesus always condemned hypocrisy in those in authority, but in the end he submitted unto them as unto his Father, even at the cost of losing his life—but it was in this that he was raised to eternal life. In death he found life. In silence he truly was heard. In obeying he came to command. If we obey those in authority, we too will come to lead others in Jesus.

June 13, 1978—3:00 P.M.*—Alverna*

Jesus brings a stability to our life. This is first an inner stability, one grounded only in his stability, one grounded in our awareness of our own instability. We must become inwardly unstable through the cross before we can come to the stability of his resurrection. We must trust only in his vision and his goal for our life if we are to be truly stable. In our instability, we will find his stability. He will rise into our life and fill us with the assurance of his plan for our life in which we will discover our purpose and our vocation.

This is also an outer stability. When Jesus calls, we follow. When he gives us a vision, we are faithful to it. This stability is an outgrowth of faith and obedience. In terms of my call to a contemplative agrarian community, this means being faithful to that community. I might embark on periodic missions from the community, but I would always return to the stability of the community upon the completion of my mission. I might even venture out to help found new communities with visions like my own, but I would always remain an outgrowth from my home community. This is simply a matter of being faithful to the vision and the call of Jesus in my life.

We live in a world of both inner and outer instability. The structure both of the family and of the local community are being destroyed, not to mention the spiritual structures of the inner man. Because of this, man himself loses the complete stability God ordained for him for his spiritual, mental, emotional, and physical well-being.

The stability of Jesus heals the entire man. Jesus provides a vision and direction by his truth and love to help the individual. He directs man back to the ordained stability in community and family structures that insure the well-being of both the individual and the family or community. In time, the reconciliation of all creation back to the stability in God is manifested through the individual and the community. Jesus desires us to be stable, for he loves us.

31

June 14, 1978—8:30 A.M.*—Alverna*

If I live the ethic of the cross in reality, I should experience a complete conversion of manners in my life. I am chaste unto my Husband because I am impregnated by his Spirit and carry his child in my womb. Now the growing of my womb is seen only because of the presence of his Spirit. My pregnancy is surely the fruit of his Spirit, which is love, joy, peace, patient endurance, kindness, generosity, faith, mildness, and chastity. His wisdom has taken hold in my very womb so that I become humble, innocent, peaceable, lenient, docile, rich in sympathy, and full of kindly and impartial deeds of sincerity. I adore only him, and worship him, for his seed now lives within me to bring me new life. I obey his wishes and humbly submit to his will in a quiet and silent spirit of meekness. I desire to be alone with my Lover in solitude at all times so that he may hold me and kiss me when I am lonely. I seek to be conformed to his mind so that we may never come to argument, separation, and divorce. Now the mind of my Husband is this: to be a slave rather than a master. To be fully human rather than a lord. To be humble rather than arrogant. To obey another rather than command. To die so that others might live, rather than defend one's self at the cost of another's death. It is because of his attitude that I love him even more than myself. In his becoming my slave, I make him my master. In his becoming fully human, I make him my Lord. In his being humble before me, I make him my exalted husband. In his choosing to obey, I have made him the giver of commands. In his choosing to die, I have let him live in me and impregnate my womb by his Spirit. Therefore, as his bride, I seek to conform my attitude to his attitude, my manner to his manner. My womb has become his womb, my body has become his body, and my child shall surely be his child. I am his lover forever and in that my manner has surely been changed.

June 14, 1978—11:30 A.M.—Alverna

Poverty, chastity, obedience, stability, and conversion of manners—Jesus has indirectly called me to these vows through his visions of my apostolate and of an agrarian community of prayer. I can vow obedience in his call to these when I understand them in light of his cross. They are not bondage to legalism. They are freedom in the way of the cross. Poverty is the wealth of the kingdom where one becomes poor so another may be rich. Chastity is the fulfillment of love that gives Jesus' name to our children. Obedience is the true way to lead others in the way of our obedient Lord. Stability is the instability of depending only on the stability of Jesus. Conversion of manners is the death of our own way in our marriage bed with Jesus, so that his way will fill our womb with humility and love when he impregnates our souls with new life in his Spirit. These vows apply ideally to all Christians, for all Christians are called to die with Jesus in the marriage bed of the cross, so that we may all rise with Jesus when his life fills our womb in pregnant expectation of new life and resurrection. Let us vow the vows of death, so we may truly know life. Let us vow the life of the cross, so that we may know his resurrection.

June 14, 1978—12:30 P.M.—Alverna

These, then, are my visions and my vows. Jesus has called me to them and I seek to respond. I have no desire to start a new religious community when so many already exist. I would much rather fit my call into the existing structure, so that humility and unity can be more clearly manifested. I share the call to silence and solitude with some of the Benedictine cenobites and the Camaldolese. I share the call to stability and conversion of manners with all the Benedictines. I share the call to poverty, chastity, and obedience with the Franciscans and most religious Orders.

I feel especially close to the joy and the freedom of St. Francis of Assisi, and I deeply respect the balance and temperance of St. Benedict. However, the lack of devotion to both gospel poverty and contemplative prayer in both of their Orders, as of late, is something that makes me very sad. You do not need a religious habit to sip on Scotch whisky or to eat a lavish feast in an expensive mansion. The habit was made for walking, not for driving an expensive car . . . or for riding a horse, for that matter. We are to be the poorest of poor men, living a life of charity and prayer. Our color television sets and expensive stereos help us accomplish neither. So while I respect the overall amount of good that both Orders do in Jesus, I seriously question whether they are always true to the vision of their founders who sought to do the greatest good humanly possible through the grace of Jesus.

I tend to respect highly those orders that zealously guard their call to poverty and contemplative prayer. The prayerful devotion of the solitary Camaldolese, the silent Trappists, and the poverty-enriched Little Brothers of St. Francis truly stir up a flame in my soul that can never be extinguished. But I could not bear the lack of the apostolate in Camaldolese or Trappist life. Nor could I continue in some of the Trappist farming techniques that strip the soil of life and bleed the yield of natural health. The Little Brothers of St. Francis are very close to the original life of Francis, which so beautifully treats the symptoms of the physical disease of this world. But I am called also to treat the cause of the physical disease of this world. So I need some contact with an agrarian community that deals with the cause of that disease by manifesting an alternative life-style that works on its own and works in harmony with nature, according to the truth of Jesus, which is his cross. The Camaldolese, the Trappists, and the Little Brothers of St. Francis all stir my heart to joy and thanksgiving, but I fear they would not accept my total vision and call from Jesus.

If they are willing to embrace my vision and my call, I am willing to embrace theirs. I desire the strength of their past, that I might meekly share their strength with the future. I would love to rest in their existing structure so that I might prepare in prayer, study, and manual labors. Then I could continue to build the temple of God upon the foundations they have already built. It would truly be a shame to start a new structure for the future, having to copy superficially the foundation of their existing structure, when I could simply build upon their foundation, so solidly built in the past and yet existing in the present. Then would the inner love and unity of the structure be more plainly manifested. Then would the structure of the future be truly strong in supporting a Christian tradition of the past. Then would the love of God's glory shine forth from this temple. I hope the existing structures will embrace me, for I long to embrace them.

Perhaps I am wrong about all of this. Perhaps many communities already exist that are called by Jesus to this vision of an agrarian Christian prayer community that periodically sends forth men in the apostolate of poverty. Perhaps they are willing to continue to come through the narrow gate of devotion so that they can see the broadening vision of an alternative Christian community that manifests the reconciliation of the cross in all areas of life. Let all of us embrace true contemplation and solitary silence, so that we might truly speak the true word of Jesus' apostolate to all the world.

June 18, 1978—5:30 P.M.—Alverna

I have felt especially close to St. Francis again this past weekend. Like myself, he was called to the contemplative and to the active apostolate life. Like myself, he came very close to choosing a strict life of solitude, silence, and prayer. Like myself, this decision was one he made after much prayer and time.

As I've indicated in past journal entries, I have felt deeply called by Jesus to the religious hermitage or contemplative prayer. In resigning myself to this solitude, I found companionship with Jesus. In resigning myself to this inner confrontation with reality and conflict, I found inner peace in his presence. In resigning myself to a life without an active apostolate, I found the contemplative life of prayer a complete fulfillment and an apostolate in itself. I could be very happy living a strictly contemplative life of solitude, silence, and prayer.

But Jesus has also called me to an apostolate of poverty and humility. In the binding poverty of Jesus, I find the freedom of his wealth. In the humility of Jesus, I also find the glory of Jesus. In giving, I receive and in forgiving others, I am forgiven. In taking a ministry that is outwardly foolish and poor, I truly reach the world with the rich wisdom of the cross.

These two calls have caused me much trial in finding God's will as a practical reality in my life. Was I to consider my past apostolate in music as the fulfillment of the apostolic call? Was I truly called to enter a strictly contemplative Order of hermits? I could do so and be very happy, for it is a life that seems very suitable to my nature in the Lord.

Two days ago, however, Jesus spoke to me again through the life of Francis. When Francis faced the same decision, God called him to preach! He was to be, first, a contemplative man of solitary prayer; second, a man of community; and third, an apostolic preacher. He was to rebuild the church through his life and his Order. It was to be the highest of all contemplative Orders, yet it was also to be the highest of all apostolic Orders of preachers and teachers. Through this example, God has reaffirmed my vocation in the apostolate of poverty. I, too, must preach the forgiving and peaceful love of Jesus to this hate-ridden world of judgment and war. The habit of the contemplative hermit is white and clean. The habit that is offered to me is a brown Franciscan habit that is worn and dirtied by the mud and dust of traveled roads. So through the life of Francis, Jesus has challenged me to the apostolate of poverty once again. Not only will I be a man of contemplative prayer, but I will also be a man of apostolic action. Thus I will follow Francis. Thus will I follow Jesus!

June 22, 1978—1:00 P.M.—Alverna

It has been an interesting couple of days. Father Martin, my spiritual mentor, has returned from Ireland. I have also visited the Benedictine monastery in St. Meinrad, Indiana. These two events have led me to think further on community and vocation.

I was looking forward to Martin's return. I wanted to share my thoughts on vocation and ask his further advice and guidance. But he and I have barely spoken. We talked some about his trip and his programs, but we never got around to discussing my need for guidance. He has been very busy and really seems to want to avoid any further "heavy discussion." I sympathize with his feeling entirely. So I have been forced to look only to the existential guidance of the Spirit to calm my soul.

I was also looking forward to visiting St. Meinrad's. I thought that the Mass I am now recording might fit nicely into their new music program. I also wanted to experience the Benedictine "vibe" in both work and worship.

I found their new music program for recording quite premature in vision and growth. I also found them hesitant to involve artists that are not part of their Benedictine community. They were all quite nice and friendly, but my present contribution to their own vision seems nonexistent due to their exclusiveness . . . but they really don't know me, so how can I truly blame their defensiveness and skepticism? I did find their directors of publishing very dynamic and sympathetic with my ideas on art, worship and reaching all denominations. In fact, I sensed that they too were limited to a degree because of the "monks on the hill." This limitation is both good and bad. But regarding music, I think they need to be more open to contemporary men and women. Only time will tell whether Jesus wants to use the positive contacts I made with these brothers.

The Benedictine "vibe" is very interesting and very much of God, but I could not relate to it vocationally. It is all very good, but in its regulated structure and its massiveness it loses the regulated freedom of a few monks living the common agrarian life of prayer. They depend mainly on Abbey Press, the gift shop. and teaching to support themselves. The simple life of a few agrarian monks seems to have been lost in the massive complexities of St. Meinrad's structure. What they do is definitely good, especially their reverent worship, but I heard God say to me, "This is not for you, John."

Today I turned to the Lord, and he was there as always. I could not find a Franciscan who was not busy. I could not find a Benedictine who was not busy. So I turned to Jesus and he found the time to talk to me.

He told me again of the community to which he has called me. He told me that this is a new call and cannot be found in existing religious Orders. He told me to be patient and to trust him, for he is going to use me to help found such a community. So today I turned only to the Lord and he was there again. I think I should talk to him more, and listen.

June 24, 1978—7:00 P.M.—Alverna

Tonight I was out praying unto the Lord. I was overcome by the Spirit as I had been at Gethsemani. Jesus gave me a staff and told me to walk the woods and sing his praises with all of creation. My brothers and sisters among the birds and the fish sang with me. The butterflies came to join in the chorus, and even brother snake came to see what the wonderful commotion was. Soon the woods were vibrating in a harmony of praise and thanksgiving unto Jesus our Creator and loving Lord.

I then felt the call to take the habit of Francis once again. I opened the Bible for guidance and my eyes came to rest on this verse in the Gospel according to St. Mark: "There is one thing more you must do. Go and sell what you have and give to the poor; then you will have treasure in heaven. After that, come and follow me."

Jesus has given me the call. I now pray for the grace to respond. Forgive me for my delay, Lord Jesus.

July 3, 1978—8:30 A.M.—*Alverna*

God has revealed some definite direction for me to follow vocationally this past week.

First, Jesus instilled a voice within me instructing me to enter the Third Order of St. Francis. This was coupled with my constantly coming across accounts of Franciscan saints who were contemplative hermits, yet were only members of the Third Order. They sometimes seemed to live a more Franciscan life than the First Order did owing to the freedom they had. I also realized the Third Order as more compatible with my community vision for lay Christians. Also, Third Order members could receive the tertiary habit as their poverty apparel, thus fulfilling my vision. So it seemed that the Third Order was potentially at least the most logical place for me to find a home; I also heard God calling me that way.

But I sought a manifestation of this call more realistically. I was holding the Franciscan Book of Saints and God told me to open it. I knew God wanted to speak to me specifically so I decided to open it to May 8th, which is my birthday. Before I opened it, I prayed that God would tell me which Order to enter and upon which kind of community life to embark. I opened and found Blessed Waldo, who was a Third Order contemplative hermit. I praised God for this. I knew Jesus was calling me to the primitive Franciscan life, but in the Third Order. A life of contemplation and solitude. A life of peace.

Next, I walked in the woods. I heard Jesus tell me to open my Bible for further guidance. I immediately opened to Mark 10:21, and Jesus' words again were, "There is one thing more you must do. Go and sell what you have and give to the poor; you will then have treasure in heaven. After that, come and follow me." The words need no explanation.

After this, I finally shared all my vocational feelings with Father Martin, my director. He agreed that God was calling me to the primitive Franciscan life of poverty and contemplation. He also agreed that I fitted most comfortably into the Third Order for now. He then commented that the next day was the feast day of Raymond Lull, who was himself an isolated Third Order member and who spent his life in an apostolate of poverty. Father Martin considered this a further "coincidence" that could be considered a sign from the Lord Jesus.

Now I wait to follow the call of Jesus. I believe God wants me to set up a community called "Charity" to fulfill the vision he gave me of a community that was like a beautiful painting of harmony. I believe God wants me to give all my possessions to this community to fulfill his word for me to free myself from all material ownership. I believe God wants me to enter the Third Order of St. Francis and live as a contemplative hermit to fulfill the vision of the habit. I believe God wants me to venture into the world, when inspired by the Spirit, in complete apostolic poverty to fulfill the vision of my apostolate.

I see the possibility of establishing a very small community of Third Order contemplatives. This community could act as a little leaven to help raise the entire loaf of new bread by manifesting the primitive apostolic life and the primitive Franciscan ideal of the gospel life. I do not see this contemplative community as the entire new loaf. It is *not* the complete alternative community of the "painting." It is simply a small group of men and women dedicated and called to the life of contemplative poverty as depicted by the gospels of Jesus. It will be a community of contemplative solitude and silence carried out in poverty, chastity, and obedience. It will be a community of prayer, dedicated to a life of continual praise and worship carried out in love. It will be the leaven for the bread of overall Christian community that threatens to fall flat for lack of exemplified contemplative prayer and praise. The community called "Charity" will manifest the dough of the new bread. This community will offer a complete alternative to the dying culture of today's world by manifesting the community of the painting. It will offer complete healing to a good world that has grown sick by selfishness and greed. It will bring the forgiving love of Jesus to our hate-ridden world that is being judged in all areas of life. In "Charity," men, women, and children will work together to bring forth the basic needs of life in harmony with God, man, and nature. A complete alternative will be manifested by living a simple life of love, concern, and compassionate forgiveness. The community will visibly offer a new birth to a dying world. Jesus forgives us and gives us a second chance. That other chance is what "Charity" will be all about.

Between the small community and the complete alternative community of my vision, a complete loaf of "living bread" will be offered to this hungry world. Jesus will feed us with his forgiving love and his guiding truth to heal us of the malnutrition of our world. Those in pain will find comfort. Those who mourn will come to rejoice. Those who die will be born again to eternal life. I pray now that I will not be too proud to receive the grace of this vision. I pray only to serve Jesus, to serve mankind, and to serve God's creation.

July 14, 1978—Alverna

Recently I have been burdened by the growing number of young adults coming to me, of all people, for help. They come from charismatic communities of both Protestant and Catholic affiliations, yet are still unfulfilled in their search for Christian community. They come from the 60's generation and so are conditioned to looking for an alternative to the world in which we live. Most see Jesus as the Source of this alternative, but have yet to see a complete alternative in his Body.

Most of these young people believe I represent *that* alternative life-style in the Body. I preach a mystical Jesus that remains practical. I preach a crucified Servant who yet remains the risen Lord. I preach a life of poverty that is the source for abundant wealth. I tell them of a solitude and silence that brings the word of our constant Companion to our heart and soul. I, quite simply, present a Franciscan interpretation of Jesus, which is both simple and deep. So it seems strange that in simply teaching them of the paradoxes of the cross of Jesus, as St. Francis did, they would think my approach "new."

These people want me to teach them for more than just one night. They want to have me stay with them for long periods of time, and some want to follow me. They come to me as their only visible hope in the Body of Christ. I do not claim to be all they say I am, but I feel I must help them if I can.

Last night I shared all of this with Father Martin. He agreed that something must be done. I suggested establishing a small lay community here at Alverna designed to train these people in the Franciscan life-style. They would live here, work here and, most importantly, live the Franciscan life here. The community would be interdenominational but would exist under the authority of the Franciscans and the Catholic Church. Those coming here could work on the grounds, in the kitchen, or in the offices in exchange for room and board. Alverna would find an inexpensive way to lighten the work load on its employees while, at the same time, fulfilling its apostolate to the world by not only teaching about community through words, but also by example. Father Martin thought the suggestion from the Lord.

July 20, 1978—9:00 A.M.*—Alverna*

What a week! Both active and contemplative. Both tiring and restful. My body is weary but my spirit is uplifted to the heavens!

I met a sister who came here for retreat. I fell deeply in love with her as a sister. Our spirits made love as we shared the value of poverty and the contemplative life of solitude and silence. The Jesus within her further impregnated my spiritual womb with love and wisdom and I now grow full from the seed he left within me.

I learned an analogy in the progress of any two lovers through this spiritual love affair. First there is much talk and conversation. In this stage the two lovers get to know each other's thoughts about life and they share personal experiences. This stage is beautiful and exciting. It is a stage that cannot be excluded from a true love relationship. Second, the lovers fall into embraces and kisses that precede the sexual act. There are few words here. Body simply touches body. The lovers feel their partner by experience rather than mere words. Gentleness, kindness, anxiety, meekness, boldness, brutality, warmth, coldness, hatred, and love are all perceived by the touching of their bodies. Heart flows into heart and lips touch lips as the relationship transcends the level of speech.

Then the woman is penetrated by the man. They both lose their individuality in this act. They are connected one to another by the most sensual and vulnerable parts of their bodies. The excitement of this union rises as they die to their selves and give life one to another. In exchange for this death to self, each lover finds the fulfillment of self as the senses rise beyond imagination and vulnerability turns to warm comfort and trust. Then the climax of the union occurs when the man and woman reach permanent union. The man leaves his life in the woman and the woman now carries part of the man's own life. They cannot be separated.

In this sexual climax, the emotional peak of the relationship is reached. The level of union is beyond mere words and is the most stimulating emotional union, but there still remains a deeper level of union for a mature couple.

This level is best likened to the afterglow of sexual union. Lover simply holds lover in trust and gentle fulfillment. Life has flowed into life. Heart knows heart. Body knows body. In this fulfilling assurance the relationship becomes quiet and peaceful. There are no words. There are no passionate embraces. There are no attempts to repeat the sexual union too quickly. There is only silence. There is only peaceful warmth. There is the final stage of love that can permeate warmth. There is the final stage of love that can permeate the lovers' entire life. It can now transcend both their speech and their sexual relationship. In knowing the communication of silence they will not become trapped by superficial words. In knowing the peaceful union of the afterglow they will not become trapped by the emotion of a merely sexual union. Communication is now beyond words and union of body and soul is even beyond emotions. The lovers now are free to face the realities of life without being bound to the necessities of a multitude of words and emotional peaks. Crisis is met with the assuredness of a true communication and constant companionship that make even solitude and silence a source for growth. The threat of docile inactivity is met by the rich assurance of growth that comes from this afterglow of truly mature lovers.

So this afterglow of gentleness and peace is the deepest union known by two lovers. It cannot be truly known without having passed through the first two stages of love. But once entered into, its unspoken communication and gentle companionship permeate and enrich any further speech or sexual union that the two lovers experience. It overcomes the crises and boredoms of a growing relationship. This is the key to a mature relationship of love.

These three stages of love apply to spiritual lovers as well as to physical lovers. For the contemplative, Jesus is the only Bridegroom, the only Lover. We must spend much time talking to him truly to understand his Word and his Will. We must pray with many sincere words that pour from our deepest heart. We must study his Word in scripture and tradition with receptive heart and mind. In this we are much like the two lovers who must first know each other through the speaking of many words. But if we are truly lovers we must go on to build a building upon the foundation of the Word. Soon the Spirit comes to touch our spirits. Soon we know him because we touch him. His touch arouses our spirits to the heights of heaven in the foreplay of our love-making. Then he penetrates the womb of our entire life when the Spirit overflows into our spirit with an excitement and an ecstasy that cannot be described by words. Surely it speaks in a language that is heard by all nations, yet cannot be limited to the confines of earthly language. His Spirit is the seed he plants within our spiritual womb in a love relationship that is truly beyond the Word and surely will grow into a newborn child when our time as his Bride is fulfilled. The last stage of the two lovers is the highest stage for the contemplative. In this stage both the intellectual communication of words and the emotional communication of sexual union are surpassed by the complete peace and union in the afterglow of sweet union between two lovers. We have learned the Word of God. We have been impregnated by the filling of the Holy Spirit. Now we simply rest in the loving arms of Jesus, ever secure as his eternal Bride and the Mother of his unborn child. We no longer feel the need to talk a lot. We no longer feel the need to make love continually. As a mature couple, we carry on a relationship that is secure and strong. Yes, we still talk by his Word sometimes. Yes, he still makes love to his Wife on special occasions. But most of the time we communicate with a love that transcends the need for continual talk and emotional rapture. We simply hold each other in an unspoken, even embrace that surely and consistently communicates our love. Wordless, unspoken, even, constant, secure, peaceful. These are the words that best describe the mature relationship between Jesus and the Mother of his children. These are the words that best describe the prayer of the mature contemplative.

August 10, 1978—9:00 P.M.*—Alverna*

Today I talked to Father Benet Fonck, the provincial assistant at Oak Brook, about the Third Order. I was extremely tired, so was unable to share my visions with any persuasive zeal. However, this was from God, for Benet proceeded to share *his* vision for the Third Order and I found it almost identical to mine! Praise God! I can be too tired to talk and still Jesus speaks the vision he gave me. This is the beauty of his Body! When I am weakest I truly discover his strength.

Like myself, Benet sees the Third Order as the home for lay people called to Franciscan community of both contemplation and action. He wants such a community in this province called a "House of Prayer" to provide: (1) a community experience of togetherness, prayer, and simple living with a core group and occasional participants where renewal may occur; (2) an opportunity to participate in continuing education programs on evangelization and spiritual growth; (3) a situation for developing a more intense life of prayer and contemplation.

I believe "Charity" could be the answer to his vision as well as mine: A Third Order community made up of a core group who work at Alverna living the contemplative life, plus a group of satellite households living an active life.

The community would emphasize prayer, study, and work together. For the core group, a contemplative daily discipline would be established consisting of prayer hours, study time, and daily labor. Satellite houses would do likewise within practical reason relative to job schedules. The entire community would meet once or twice a week for sharing, study, and prayer. The community would reach out to all Christians and all faiths in evangelistic programs that share the teachings of the cross of Jesus as the source for true resurrection in life. These programs would both be sent out to other local areas and be given at Alverna.

"Charity" would be a working Franciscan lay community, existing to share the Franciscan concept of community with a world that is hungry for the bread of living community. It would share not just by words, but also by its very existence. Thus will the true alternative of Jesus' love be manifested to this hate-ridden world. The community would be truly Franciscan. The community would be Catholic. Yet the community would also be interdenominational. Thus will the community be of Jesus.

August 12, 1978—4:00 P.M.— Gethsemani, Ky.

Today I seek only to disappear in the cross of Jesus and never to be found again. Thus will only Jesus be found in my resurrection. I pray this life of activity to which God has brought me recently will lead me eventually to such an end of contemplation. I hope the activity of founding the Third Order community will lead its members to a life of solitary and silent prayer, study, and work. Then will we rest in contemplative peace. So I pray, Lord Jesus, that this desire you have given me may be granted in your own good time. Please, let me be nothing so you may be all in all.

But why, God, have you called me to be both a hermit and a teacher? Why both a follower and a founder? Why both a lover of silence and a proclaimer of words? My deepest heart sought only to follow a life of solitude, silence, and prayer as taught by the established religious Orders. Yet those I follow in these Orders tell me to help found a new community by venturing into the world and spreading the gospel by words and singing. Thus I know that you, too, have called me to such a life. I am frightened to lead and speak! I have not yet learned humility and obedience. God save me from pride and lusting for power. God save me, for I am scared.

August 12, 1978—7:00 P.M.— Gethsemani

I have spent some time rereading the Rule of St. Benedict for the "I don't know how manyeth time" today. I am again struck by the need for a community daily discipline. I am convinced that discipline nurtures a holy life of contemplative prayer if that discipline is living and breathing by the breath of God. Discipline in prayer, study, and labor brings forth bountiful crops that are sweet to the taste of her sower (Sirach 6:18–20). She seems burdensome to the unruly fool, but to the wise and obedient the burden of her way is soon found to be the source of rest and joy (Sirach 6:22–29). So let us discipline our body through labors of watchings, fastings, and charities. Thus, through the bearing of these burdens, our life will become substantially free of all unrighteousness and evil inclinations. May the Lord be praised, who is the giver of all true wisdom and discipline.

In "Charity," I am inclined to believe a strict discipline of life should be adopted by the core group of contemplatives. This will require more dedication of her members, but this also insures the seriousness of their commitment to both "Charity" and Jesus. Thus will "Charity" fly freely in the Spirit who brings true contemplative peace.

August 13, 1978—10:00 A.M.— Gethsemani

God has revealed that I am to use this retreat to draw up a general discipline for the proposed Third Order community at Alverna. This rule will be fairly comprehensive yet very open for flexibility. It will be designed to give a concrete discipline by which an individual can live the Franciscan life at various levels, yet still maintain a unified community. Flexibility is very, very important, yet a strict discipline is the key for community survival; discipline guards, defends, and strengthens a prayerful and contemplative spirit. Most of all, I pray that the Spirit of Jesus will anoint my thinking and my writing to help those called by the Spirit to the Franciscan life of gospel poverty, penance, and prayer. Thus will our apostolic ministry flower from the vine of contemplative prayer in Jesus.

August 13, 1978—1:00 P.M.*—* *Gethsemani*

During lunch we heard a teaching on the agony of Jesus in Gethsemane. There Jesus died to his own will in obedience to the will of the Father. He cried in sorrow and shame for the sins of mankind. He fell prostrate before the Father under the agony of this burden of man's sin. He gave his own lifeblood for our life as he sweat beads of blood in this intercessory agony. His love for us caused him to be hated. His desire for our comfort caused him to suffer agony both in the garden and on the cross. So a share in the love of Jesus truly causes one to suffer. In this suffering we share in the life of Jesus, our Lord and example.

During this teaching, many references to the Holy Land were made. Once again I felt Jesus calling me to walk in his own footsteps there. I feel it is in Jerusalem that I will truly come to know the cross of Jesus. He will teach me of his agony there by my being there. Then can I comfort with his resurrection those dying in Israel. Then can I pray the Peace Prayer of Francis even where Francis first prayed it. Then may I bring the peace of Jesus to a war-torn people.

I have, here at Gethsemani, as at St. Meinrad, heard the voice of Jesus. He calls me to a Franciscan vocation more and more as time progresses. I desire the discipline of the Cistercian and Benedictine, but not at the expense of losing the flexible freedom and joy of the Franciscan. I seek the death of the cross which is living resurrection. I seek to be impregnated at the cross, so that I might freely and naturally grow full in the love of Jesus in order to bear the children of God. It requires discipline, most definitely, for the woman to care for herself properly and her unborn child during her pregnancy, but pregnancy and birth are very natural processes. They will usually come along all right with or without discipline. However, for the sake of unknown dangers, discipline is assumed to guide the natural process as its strong defender. So discipline serves natural freedom. Freedom does not serve discipline.

August 14, 1978—10:45 A.M.— *Gethsemani*

Alverna is calling me in her simple freedom and vast potential for action and solitary contemplation. I am ready to leave Gethsemani and go to her once more. She is my home now.

August 18, 1978—2:20 P.M.— *Chicago's O'Hare Airport*

I have been doing some thinking concerning the foundations of spiritual poverty and humility as they apply to my apostolate. An apostolate dependent upon secular foundations cannot stand when the sea of heavenly water rushes about it. It is one thing for Christians to "make tents" like St. Paul while ministering, but it is quite another to make the ministry itself totally dependent on "tentmaking."

If your ministry is not strong enough to stand by itself, then you should simply become a Christian "tentmaker." There is nothing wrong with that, for you will still minister the love of Jesus in a secular setting. However, you should not say you emphasize ministry, when in truth you must emphasize and depend on "tentmaking" in order to exist. You should not think to yourself, "They come to me because of my ministry," when in truth they come to you because of your "tents." Oh, they may appreciate your ministry, but they come because of your "tents." If this is the case, then simply call yourself a Christian "tentmaker" and perform your task as unto the Lord.

One must now deal with the common American concept of advertising. Scripture tells the humble man never to praise himself, but always to let another's lips praise you. This is quite different from the accepted advertising methods of our American culture. As a capitalist nation, the concept of competition is inbred into us as a "good" thing. Competition means we must push ourselves to the top and push others to the bottom. In advertising, this means we must boast of our accomplishments and praise ourselves loudly, so as to let everyone know that we are "better" than our competitors. This concept must be regarded by Christians as alien to the "advertising campaigns" of the humble, religious man. In fact, for the humble follower of Jesus, these attitudes and actions must be considered "bad" or "evil."

Even the advertising concept of simply publishing the truth of your accomplishments is alien to the way of our humble Lord. Jesus' accomplishments were always published by others. The people whom he touched, healed, and loved were the ones who told the world of his "better" way. His way was, in fact, "better." Jesus himself knew that his way was "better." But as our model of exalted humility, Jesus himself never attempted to publicize his way. It was simply because his way was "better" that his way was publicized among the people, despite his humble efforts to stop them, and finally thousands flocked to him when he appeared in public. It was, in fact, his love and his humility that made his healings so appealing to the crowds. If Jesus would have publicized his healings himself, then he would have gone against his humility, and his ministry would have become powerless in the end.

For those involved in Christian ministry, this means that we may advertise the "better" way of Jesus as humble truth, but we must never advertise our own accomplishments in him. Jesus faithfully told the world of the Father, but he was humble and silent regarding the "making public" of his own glory. Thus did the Father choose to glorify the Son. Likewise, we must imitate the humility of Jesus if we are to taste of his glory. So let the Christian minister speak loudly of the accomplishments of Jesus himself in others, but he must let another praise the accomplishments of Jesus in himself.

Even the "tentmaker" must follow Jesus' humility if he says he knows of Jesus' glory. He may tell the world that he is a tentmaker. He may even tell the world how he makes his "tents." He may also display the "tents" he makes. But let him never speak of his "tents" as "better" than another's. Let him never say he is a "good" tentmaker. Let him simply remain in humble silence when it comes to praising his own work or his own talent. If he is good, then the people will know. If they know, then they will praise the quality of his talent and his work. Upon hearing this praise, the people will listen more closely to his humble advertising. Upon hearing this praise, the people will listen more closely to his words about the love and humility of the Jesus he follows.

As one who seeks to be involved in pure ministry, the above points have many implications. I must build my ministry without relying on my "tentmaking" or my mystical talents to attract the crowd. I must build my ministry without boastful advertisements regarding either my success as a minister or my success as a musician. I must simply sing unto the Lord and speak the word of his healing grace in poor humility so that others might glorify the riches of the Lord in me. If I minister well, those who should hear me will be called by God through the praises of others. They won't come because I am a well-known musician, although I hope they enjoy my music; they will come because I minister the simple love of Jesus in the pattern of his humility.

This means that the music I produce must be worship music—music that directs the thoughts of the listener only toward Jesus. The music of the Christian should be played as skillfully as possible, but the paradox of strength in weakness will also be evident if the truth of the cross is to be fully manifested. This means that those with skill and those without skill must join together in a harmony of voices to manifest the true strength of Christ—the strength of unity and acceptance in love regardless of race, sex, state of life, or talent. This means that we will worship God as a unified people. This means that the music I produce must lend itself toward group participation. This means I will be a "liturgist." If my ministry is dependent on the secular, technical aspects of my solo musicianship, then my ministry has somehow been directed away from the way of Jesus. If it knowingly nurtures an attitude that produces a scene of Christian "rock stars," then I must not be so bold as to call my approach "Christ-like." My music should be skillful, but it should be entirely centered on worship. People may enjoy my skill, but my skill should help only to lead others into worship. I should never rely solely on my technical skill to carry forth my ministry; and if I become involved in a movement that looks to my solo skill before they look to unity into the Lord, then I will purposely subdue my musical skills so that true unity of worship might be the center of my music.

There is nothing wrong with soloists recording artistic Christian musical liturgies. Comtemporary artistic liturgies are needed in the church, and records are a good way to educate the people of the church about their beauty and legitimacy. However, these albums must be recorded in humility and poverty as worship and released only to lead people into the wealth and exaltation of worship. This is the essence of the true artist, for only through worship can the true, naked soul be exposed; and only in communication of the naked soul can art be true. But true art as worship can only be true worship when the paradoxical way of the cross, the unity of the church, and the reality of mankind and Jesus are manifested. Therefore, these albums may be artistically and skillfully recorded, but the aim of recording these albums is to manifest the naked soul's true worship of God in Jesus. We are not recording to impress the listener with individual talent as secular recordings do. If we do this, we have not fulfilled in Christ our purpose for being as artists and liturgists. We are here to communicate humbly and to expose the poor, naked soul of mankind. We are here to be true artists and liturgists. We are here to join together truthful worship of the exalted Giver of all glory and all wealth—Jesus the Christ.

As far as letting people know about my ministry through advertising, I must, once again, do so only if humility and poverty can be preserved. I have no problem with sending out simple announcements about what I do, how I do it, and that I am available to serve a community. I have no problem with humbly telling people who I am if they want to know. I have no problem with showing people what I look like and what my average audiences look like if they want to know. But may I never boast of my past or present talents and accomplishments! Let me never try to impress a potential sponsor with my drawing power! To do this I would have to praise my own accomplishments in music, ministry, and entertainment. This I simply cannot do if I call myself a follower of Jesus. Let me never spend huge amounts to finance a huge advertising campaign designed to impress the public with the superior talents in both music and ministry of "John Michael Talbot!" Let the advertising I use only be used if the humility and poverty of the cross may be preserved. Thus will my ministry go forth in the power of the risen Lord!

August 19, 1978—1:00 to 2:00 P.M.— *Plane to Vancouver*

I simply seek to forget my past and my future so that I can give my all to the praising of God today. I sometimes feel I have not really died yet. I sometimes feel that the John Michael Talbot of the past is still alive and kicking and trying to invade both my present and future under the guise of "contemporary music ministry."

All this talk and thought about the "ethics of ministry" . . . I pray that we do not rationalize our secular tendencies. It is easy to maneuver words of theology to fit your cause. I have done it many times before. It is easy to "Christianize" secular endeavors and buildings without really changing the substance of the foundation. You simply paint Jesus' name all over the building, then everyone takes it for granted that it is his building. But what really makes a building Christian is when Jesus himself has changed the actual substance of the building materials used and then gone on to build a new building himself. The old building must be torn down so Jesus can build a new edifice where the old one once stood. This is the teaching of the cross and the resurrection.

I say this only because of the visions Jesus has given me for my new life and ministry. This life and ministry are both Franciscan and monastic. He has held out the tattered habit of St. Francis to me and told me to live a life of solitude, silence, and prayer. At the same time, he has called me to a walking apostolate of absolute poverty and humility. He has called me to the Third Order to fulfill my vision for lay community.

So I must now follow. Enough of this cowardly humanistic rationalization of his call! I must simply follow and trust in God. When St. Francis was told to rebuild the church, he simply began to rebuild churches. He did not try to rationalize God's call. This was the beauty of St. Francis's simple and childlike obedience and faith. Granted, Jesus had much more in mind, but it was only by Francis following the call in simple trust of its literal meaning that he was able to go on and fulfill its symbolic meaning. It was his childlike simplicity that caused him to fulfill the vision in depth and maturity. Without the simple response, the deep conclusion was impossible.

In the same way, when Jesus called the first disciples, they simply followed. They left their homes and their businesses to follow

Christ. They did not try to rationalize and plan, fitting the ministry to their business . . . they simply followed. They trusted Jesus enough to leave the care of their families and themselves to Jesus alone. It was because of this simple faith in the literal meaning of "follow me" that they went on to be the builders of a great church. Without this first step of faith, they would not have been counted worthy enough to be the primary builders of the church of Jesus. In leaving their secure businesses totally behind them to follow the poverty of Jesus, they went on to build the kingdom of God on earth and gain eternal life.

So I now seek only obedience to his call to follow him to the cross. I seek only to be clothed in the poor man's habit. I seek the life of the solitary hermit and the poverty-stricken preacher. Let my life be a life of solitary prayer and silence. Let my apostolate be carried forth in the poverty of this world's poor. Then will Christ clothe me in the glory of his kingdom. Then will I have constant companionship with him. Then will my apostolate of poverty be mightier than the mightiest crusades of this world's greatest and richest kings. Then will the fruit of both my life and my ministry live in eternal resurrection.

To conclude this whole line of thought, let me say this: If I must use the secular foundation of competitive and boastful advertising and constant album releases to build my ministry, then it is time for me to leave my so-called "ministry." If this is the case, then it is time to tear down the secular remains of my past building and let Jesus' call to both a life of solitude and poverty be the foundation of the building of my new life.

If I cannot be both humble and poor while remaining in my present ministry, then I cannot remain there. Jesus alone, and the state of life he has called me to, must be the foundation of the building of my new life and new ministry in him. Any other foundation I try to use will crumble under the weight of the temptations of the modern world of excessive materialism and prideful competition. In order that my life and my ministry might be a strong building that can stand amidst the bombs and earthquakes of this world's

56

materialism and competitive pride, let me build upon the foundation of Jesus' call to live a life of humility and poverty. Let me follow him into solitude to worship the Father, and let me follow him into the world to preach the wealth of the kingdom. But let me follow him also in his humility and poverty. Only then will I be able to taste of his constant companionship in solitude, his exalted glory in humility, and the eternal wealth of his kingdom in poverty. Only then will I be able to share my Companion, my Glory, and my Wealth with all the world. Only then will the building of my life and my ministry stand strong when all others fall to the ground in weakness. Let my ministry be one of humility and poverty, or let it be nothing at all!

August 24, 1978—8:00 P.M.*—Alverna*

My ministry must be an extension of my being. My being must not be dependent on my ministry; my ministry must be dependent on my being.

This means that my existence must be substantially self-sufficient without relying unduly on my music ministry for support.

This has many effects on my call to the contemplative life of solitude, poverty, and prayer. I must be able to get by on next to nothing so that I might be free for the contemplative work of prayer and the active work of ministry. A small hermitage with wood heat, one light, and hand-pumped water would cut my expenses way down. An occupation of gardening for Alverna would supply me with basic food and the right to use their bathroom facilities if I cannot build my own. This would be a primitive existence of poverty, humility, and manual labor, but the richness of this solitude and this freedom would nurture a life of contemplative prayer. Thus would my ministry truly be an extension of my being, rather than vice versa.

I began to check around Alverna in search of building materials.

I soon found some old bricks and stones I could use if I cleaned and moved them myself. Brother Paul told me of a spring that was readily available only a few feet below the spot I chose for this hermitage. I discovered some old oil drums that could be easily converted into a wood-burning heater. All in all, just about everything I would need for my hermitage of poverty and solitude were readily available on the Alverna grounds. All I had to do was beg the use of them and the "place" from the Friars.

I now began to realize just how "Franciscan" this whole leading was. Like Francis, I must begin my vocation begging stones. Like Francis, I must beg the use of land from an established religious Order. Like Francis, this place was connected with devotion to Mary. Like Francis, I must first seek a life of poverty and solitude before I could dare venture to share the wealth of the kingdom of heaven among the multitude of men upon the earth.

I also talked to Paul about doing limited manual labor at Alverna. He said that I was free to undertake extensive gardening projects if I were serious enough to see them through. He also said this would be sufficient work to justify the food and water I would use. Once again, like Francis, I could do lowly manual labor in exchange, not for money, but for the basics of food, clothing, and shelter.

August 24, 1978—10:00 P.M.*—Alverna*

In talking to Father Martin about all of this, he said only "Amen." He, too, felt that my ministry should be an outreach of my "being" and that my "being" should be that of a contemplative hermit. He thought my plans for the hermitage were in keeping with the Franciscan vision in its primitive years, and were much needed in our sophisticated modern times.

So now I wait to embark on my vocation. I seek the wealth of poverty and the companionship of solitude. I seek an active ministry built only on the foundation of contemplative peace. I intend to take the worn-out habit held out to me by God with humble courage. I intend to build my hermitage with my own hands on the ground donated by a religious Order with stones I have begged. I intend to build my hermitage under the intercession of Mary, who is both my sister and my mother. Then I will follow the example of St. Francis in supporting a church built by Jesus. I intend to be conformed to the image of Jesus on the cross in all areas of this life. Then will I know the image of our glorified Lord in heaven.

August 26, 1978—4:30 P.M.*—Sacramento*

I long to be free of the folly of this life. Who are we? What are we? I see row after row of crackerbox houses and wonder "why?" We toil and work all our lives in the name of "progress" and end up in a crackerbox house with a self-consuming existence that eventually eats us alive. Our TVs and radios keep telling us that this is the "good life," but deep inside we all doubt their confident-sounding assurance, for we know we are being eaten alive. Modern society has made life extremely complex in the quest for happiness, but we all remain unfulfilled. I think of my happy little life at Alverna and realize that only a life of simple prayer can ever fulfill me personally. I need only food, clothing, and shelter for the flesh and prayer for the spirit. In these things alone do I find my reason for being and my fulfillment. It is my relationship with our simple Jesus that is my peace and my joy. It is to this end I have been created, and it is only to this end that I truly and fully come to be.

August 30, 1978—6:30 P.M.*—Los Angeles*

I have had a great time with my brothers and sisters. The Holy Spirit is filling his people with simple love to prepare them for the work of unity he is now beginning. We are learning the exaltation of humility and the consolation of consoling others. We must learn to bend to one another in understanding and compassion if our tree is to remain intact when the strong winds come. If we do not bend in humility, then we will surely break into pieces from stiff pride. If we do not bend our backs under the weight of the humility of the cross, we will never stand upright in the glorious resurrection. We are learning the strength of bending.

But I must also say I am wearied by a fellowship of many words. I grow tired of *talking* about worship. I would much rather simply *worship*. I grow tired of *talking* about music. I would much rather simply *make music*. I grow tired of *talking* about humility and love. I would rather simply *serve* in humility and love. I grow tired of *talking* about "being" a Christian. I would much rather just *"be."*

August 31, 1978—2:00 P.M.— Jackson, Miss.

I also feel drained due to some of my secular activities in L.A. These activities deal mainly with leisure time. I am not used to watching a lot of TV or listening to a lot of rock 'n roll any more. I must say that I found these activities detrimental to my contemplative work. Since abstaining from these things, I have found I really enjoy them in moderation while ministering to people who are used to them. But when made a part of my personal daily routine, I found them to be spiritually detrimental. I feel it is because they minister almost exclusively to my flesh. Rock 'n roll ministers to the flesh by its "groove." Television ministers to the flesh by its constant "action." Consequently, the flesh "feeds" off these things and grows very strong. The activities of the flesh (at least from my own experience) are like a fat man's stomach. It cannot be satisfied. The more you feed it, the stronger its own hunger becomes.

60

Soon this hunger begins to overtake the spirit and cries loudly whenever its "food" is removed. I am now convinced that the flesh should receive only what it needs for a slim and trim existence in order that the spirit can live in the abundant luxury of the spiritual kingdom.

From my trip to L.A. and my discussion with Sparrow Records President Billy Ray Hearn, I have also concluded that most Christian contemporary music is simply "Christianized" rock 'n roll. It is simply secular music without the offensive *lyrics* of the world. Now we must understand that most people don't usually listen to the lyrics when they listen to popular music. They listen to the rhythm, the chords, and the melodies. Even with Christian contemporary music, most day-to-day listeners seldom hear the lyrics when they play an album. They are usually attracted by the physical things of the music such as rhythms and melodies. However, with the omission of offensive lyrics, a Christian is free to listen without blatant obstacles to enjoying the music. For the most part, Christian contemporary music is a way for Christians to enjoy the physical aspect of American contemporary music without the offense of having to hear American contemporary lyrics.

I think this has its good points and its bad points. I must be extremely careful not to say this aspect of Christian contemporary music is exclusively one or the other, lest I judge my brothers' and sisters' ministries and thus judge the Lord who gave them their ministries. I think this is good for a couple of reasons. First, this kind of music meets people where they are. It meets the man of modern culture *through* modern culture. The Christian musician is able to be what he is before the Lord and church by playing unto the Lord and the church with a music that he has known all his life. Likewise, the Christian listener is able to hear music he truly enjoys that also speaks of the love of our Lord Jesus. So just as Jesus met people on their own turf while he walked this earth, he continues to do so today through his church's use of Christian contemporary music.

Second, it gives the Christian of modern culture a light alternative entertainment which requires little effort to enjoy. Modern men and women are used to relaxing with secular entertainment. Music serves as such a tool because it allows the mind to rest while the body enjoys the soothing melody and the grooving. The modern Christian will usually not totally abstain from such a tool for relaxation; it is too much a part of him. So, by "Christianizing" this secular tool, the modern Christian is free to use this tool in moderation without doing serious harm to his spiritual walk.

The danger of this type of music deals mainly with concentrating on it exclusively as the only effective contemporary style. There are two main reasons for my saying this. First, Christian music has the potential of being something new to this world as a legitimate art form. It is truly a "new song." It is like a beautiful building that God alone has inspired us to build, one unique from all other buildings in this world. The materials used to build it are the materials of divinely inspired creation and Christlike love. We will produce creative music by choirs and groups that may be sung by *a loving unity* of both the talented and untalented congregation, as we lead them in true worship. Thus will the God of the creation of the universe and the God of the love of the cross be manifested in our music. Thus will the new creation of unity be manifested by the "new song" of the church. And, as I have said before in this journal, only in worship does art truly reach its potential as a communicator of the naked human soul.

But it is not enough to have only the material for a building if you wish to construct it effectively. You must also have the tools with which to construct it if the job is to be done correctly. I believe that these tools are a working knowledge of all musical styles of the past in mankind's history. We must understand which type of music best communicates different types of human experience if we are fully to communicate the wide variety of emotions encompassed in the true worship experience. It is true that no one person will come to this complete knowledge in this life, but we must all learn to our capacity if we are to be good cobuilders with Jesus in the building of the new "musical mansion." The more we open ourselves to the complete spectrum of materials and tools available to us, the more participation we will have with Jesus in the actual building of this new musical mansion.

This in no way belittles what involvement we do have as Christian contemporary popular musicians, but a narrow approach keeps us from the potential involvement we could have if we opened ourselves to the vast storehouse of materials and tools available to us in the classics of the past. I believe that Christian contemporary music is in danger of limiting its involvement in this total vision of a "new musical mansion" by using only a limited number of available materials and tools. We emphasize "quality" almost to the point of excluding congregational participation, but at the same time we limit our use of styles to contemporary, country, jazz, folk, and rock simply because we are too busy to investigate the true classics or ethnic folk sources. This is a contradiction! True quality can come only by opening ourselves to a wide variety of classics and having the God-given discipline to master their techniques for communicating the human emotion of the naked soul. True congregational participation can come only when the music is of the quality to touch the listener's naked soul, and thus prompt him to join and sing in worshipful praise of God our Creator and Redeemer. Christian contemporary music needs to expand into new musical and spiritual areas if it is to participate fully with the Master Builder in the building of this "new musical mansion" of liturgical worship.

The second danger of today's trend in contemporary Christian music lies in limiting itself to a style that still appeals mainly to man's flesh. If, because of the musical style, the listener attends only to the rhythm and melody, without going on to listen to the lyric and enter into worship, the music is actually contributing to the spiritual stagnation of the listener. As I have said earlier, this music has an incredibly valid place with the Christian of today's world, especially the new convert just learning to walk with the Lord; but if we do not also offer the listener something beyond this elementary stage of Christian worship music, then we do not lead the listener fully into worship. As a matter of fact, we actually contribute to the feeding of his flesh, which can eventually destroy the spirit if it is allowed to grow too strongly undisciplined. We have a responsibility to nurture the spirit of humanity if we are to be liturgists involved in music that is truly worship. Our music must appeal mainly to the spirit and mind of man. To put it in liturgical terms, "the music must serve the message." This message is a message of naked spirit and selfless love. Thus will our art be true art. Thus will our music be truly Christian.

In speaking to Billy Ray about his involvement with my new liturgical Mass, I must conclude the following at this point: I feel led to Billy Ray, but not as much to Sparrow itself. Sparrow is going in the direction of commercial Christian contemporary music that deals mainly in contemporary styles of music. This is not bad, but I believe it is limiting as it concerns the total vision for a "new musical mansion." Billy Ray is a man I deeply respect both spiritually and musically. He is a true man of God. He is also very interested in bridging the gap between Catholic and Protestant contemporary musical efforts, and feels we have a lot to share with one another, both musically and spiritually. I agree with this wholeheartedly. But in order for my involvement with him to be "right," we would have to share the vision for this "new musical mansion." I could not help him reach only the Catholic believers so that he could enlighten them about the Christian rock 'n roll of Sparrow Records. This would border on exploitation. I personally believe mature Catholics have gone beyond the need for such music, with the possible exception of the youth involved in the charismatic renewal. I believe Billy Ray must be willing to put energy into a whole new thrust of music and spiritual creativity if my possible involvement with him is to be in keeping with the complete call of God to today's contemporary musicians. Perhaps a completely new label dealing with a new quality of creative liturgy would be in order. Oh well, time will tell. For now, I can only say that something within me feels good about Billy Ray Hearn, while something within me is cautious about my own personal involvement with Sparrow. I am compatible with the man, but not yet with his company.*

September 1, 1978—12:00 Noon— Meridian, Miss.

The reason I have gone into all this about the marketing of liturgical music is that the "who and what" of my "I am" must be set in order before I can fully enter into the contemplative work of simply being "that" I am. In the spiritual walk of contemplation we must first understand the cross in view of our sin. In true penance we must turn from our sin daily with humble and contrite hearts. Our sin must die daily on the cross with Jesus if we are to be daily resurrected in the righteousness of Jesus. This is the first and most important step in the spiritual walk. Secondly, we must apply the ethic of the cross vocationally. How does the cross apply to the practical "who and what" we are in day-to-day life? What is our office in the church? How do we make a living? What is our true capacity of ministering the love of Jesus to the world? All of these things are important questions to the contemplative. They must be answered before the contemplative can enter into the highest stage of contemplative peace with a sure and settled mind. This highest stage is the stage of simply being "that" you are. This stage is entered into by the man who is peacefully assured in his calling. He is sure of his sin and his redemption in Jesus. He is sure of his vocation. Now he can simply come before Jesus and be what he is. Now the contemplative work is left uncluttered of the questions and doubts about sin and vocation. Now the contemplative can enter into the arms of his Lover without having to worry about having left something unfinished in the "house."

*With the release of "The Lord's Supper" in 1979, a new worship label, "Birdwing," created by Sparrow Records, was to carry most of John Michael's new kind of music.

65

I would like to compare this to a husband and wife who desire to have a romantic evening alone. In order for the evening to be perfect, they must make sure that both the house and the children are taken care of so neither will interrupt their solitary evening of romantic love. They must be free to give themselves wholly to each other without having reserved thoughts about the household. These thoughts will inhibit their love relationship and ruin the purpose of the evening. If the household is not in order, their love will be hindered even on a day-to-day basis. When the woman is sure of her calling in the home, then the love relationship between her and her husband prospers without hindrance, and will actually become a strength in dealing with the problems that might arise in day-to-day life.

I am like the wife who must get her household in order. I know I am the Husband's wife. We have even brought forth many children as an outgrowth of our love. But my household is not entirely what it was called to be. I know that until it is placed in perfect order, my Husband will not have my perfect and whole attention when we experience love. The relationship will be very good as it was in the past, but it will not be what it could be potentially. So now I seek to set my household in better order so that my Husband and I may enter freely into the contemplative heights of a mature marital love relationship. I seek to be silently held in the arms of my Husband. I seek only the love of my Jesus.

September 2, 1978—5:00 A.M.*—Meridian*

Today, I have a strong desire simply to "be." It has wearied me to feel as if I must actively tell an audience about my relationship with Jesus in order to exist. It seems as if my existence on the road is centered on this activity. All the relationships I build with others are built upon a foundation of my ability to talk about Jesus. I seek a life of simply "being" in Jesus. A life that naturally provides for my basic needs and speaks in itself of my being in Jesus

. . . a life centered on contemplative prayer with Jesus and active charity in Jesus . . . a life impregnated by the Spirit of Jesus that quite naturally brings forth children. I am tired of being looked upon as one who induces labor. I say that we should let the children be born naturally from the wombs of the normal day-to-day lives of those impregnated by the Holy Spirit. Let the pregnancy be complete in mature fruits of love, lest the child be born prematurely and be forced to live in an incubator as its unnatural environment. Without the incubator a premature child will often die; so let us stop forcing labor unnecessarily upon mothers who have yet to grow in the fullness of the love of Christ. Let us grow full daily in the love of Jesus so that we might naturally bring forth children of love when our pregnancy has matured. Today I look forward to going home where I can simply "be" as I must "be." This is the way I will be the best mother to my children. This is the way I will be the best wife to my Husband. This is the way I will be the best Christian.

September 6, 1978—9:00 P.M.*—Alverna*

I began work on the hermitage. It is the hardest work I have done in a good long while, at least since my "organic gardening" days of several years ago. I dug into the hillside several feet, having to move about five small trees and their not-so-small root systems. I also dug down six or so feet before hitting the underground spring for my cistern. I must say that it has been fitting that I began work on the hermitage on Labor Day when the reading in the epistle for the day said, "If you do not work, you will not eat." It struck me that if I am to eat of the "living bread" off the "table" of contemplative solitude, I must first work very hard at constructing a hermitage for the community.

I must also go on with my plans to arrange my life without becoming self-centered in my actions. I pray that all I do will simply be done to increase my own spiritual and physical poverty in order that others may know the wealth of the kingdom through my life and my ministry. May my own drinking never be done at the expense of denying anyone else his cup of living water.

May my own eating never be done at the expense of denying anyone else his portion of the living bread. May I rather learn to fast so others may be fed. May the wealth I find in poverty never lead to impoverishing those of earthly wealth from the wealth of the heavenly kingdom. Then will I live in the love of Jesus. Then will I reign in the power of the King of Kings.

September 7, 1978—6:30 A.M.*—Alverna*

I am considering entering into the Third Order tonight, the eve of the feast day of Mary's birth, and also the eve of Raymond Lull's description day in the Franciscan Book of Saints. Raymond Lull was a divorced man with a little girl; he also felt the call to become a Franciscan. Because of his state in life, he became a Third Order lay brother. He spent nine years in contemplative solitude before actually embarking on his active preaching and teaching apostolate. He is best remembered by his apostolate of writing and preaching. My similarity with him in calling is almost uncanny. My being led to both him and Blessed Waldo is something I feel to be of the Lord. I am also feeling the presence of Mary becoming important in my life. I feel that she really does love me and intercedes to God on my behalf. She is both a good mother and a good sister to me. She understands my heart that seeks to know the joy of resurrection by sharing the piercing sorrow of the death of her own Son. So by the intercession of Mary, Francis, Raymond, and Waldo may I enter the Third Order and begin my life of contemplative adoration of the heavenly King of Peace and active sharing of his kingdom on earth. May Jesus, who teaches us all how to intercede in love, watch over me as I seek to live the life of the gospel in a fuller way than in my past.

September 8, 1978—Alverna

I entered into the Third Order of St. Francis on the eve of this day. The ceremony was simple and sweet. In fact, it was over before I realized its significance. But afterward God anointed me heavily with the Spirit of Jesus. I began to feel the call to the cross in a very intense way. My heart became warm with repentance and my eyes wet with tears as I realized the significance of this step in my vocational life and my failure to respond fully. My call to poverty was not just a matter of charity and love; it had now become a matter of simple obedience. Jesus had directly called me to follow only after I had sold all that I owned and given to the poor. Only then would I gain the treasures of heaven. I truly felt as if I had failed in obeying the direct word of the Lord Jesus.

This morning I confessed this fault to Father Martin. I told him that I realized all Christians, or even all Franciscans, did not have to dispose of all their material possessions to be poor in the spirit of gospel poverty. I simply felt that Jesus had called me with a personal call, and I had been slothful in answering it. Oh, I had every intention of responding. But my response was becoming more vague as I clouded the issue with my own rationalizations concerning the "real world." Well, the only "real world" I seek is the real world of Jesus. I seek only the heavenly kingdom. So now I seek to turn from my sloth by actively seeking to follow the call of Jesus—a call to strict poverty for the sake of the kingdom of heaven.

I still see that I really have few possessions. I own only clothing, books, guitars, a van, and some land in Arkansas. All I have exists for the benefit of my ministry. The books for my education. The guitars for my music. The van for transportation in connection with my ministry. The land for use by a future lay community. I am simply not living in selfish luxury. I use nothing for personal gain. Then why this call to rid myself of all possessions?

I must rid myself of unnecessary possessions because while they supposedly exist for the ministry, they actually inhibit the ministry by the financial debt incurred through their very existence. For instance, by owning a van and paying insurance to transport my ministry legally, my ministry is forced to operate every month in order to pay for these "ministry aids." I must minister regularly in order to pay for the things I acquired supposedly to free the ministry. But actually, the ministry quickly becomes theoretically self-devouring in this vicious circle of financial bondage. So, by ridding the ministry of these "aids," the ministry will be free to fly under the sole inspiration and guidance of the wind of the Spirit. I will be free to give the gift I have received as a gift to others. If a church wants me to share my gift with them, I should be able to go if they can simply get me there. My personal monthly expenses should then be lower without a van and insurance; so my need to bring money home will be less. This means I could also be more selective as to which ministry comes in "under" in a local area. However, this is an entirely different subject that I will discuss later. For now, let me simply say, "I seek to free the ministry of undue financial burdens."

September 9, 1978—2:45 P.M.*—Alverna*

The Arkansas land is another matter. I acquired this land five years ago with a community in mind. The land does not aid my apostolate in song; it exists only for the benefit of my apostolate in establishing Christian community. Nonetheless, the monthly payments for the land are made by the money I bring in from the music ministry. Therefore, the music ministry must go forth every month in order to make these payments on the land that will serve another ministry. Thus, the music ministry is bound, once again, with a financial burden that it does not truly need in order to exist. The question must be asked: is it right to bind a ministry to a financial debt that is not necessary for the existence of the ministry? Is it right to force a ministry into an activity involving inferior circum-

70

stances simply to pay a bill that is not even paid toward the existence of the ministry? I do not think so! I think this binds the source ministry with unnecessary financial chains and could possibly compromise the purity of the ministry with impure local circumstances. The source ministry could be forced to go forth into an immature, sponsoring, local ministry for purely financial motives unless the source ministry is free of all unnecessary financial responsibilities.

If the Arkansas land payment exists for a community ministry, yet is dependent on the music ministry for a source of finances, then I believe it must find another source for income. Otherwise, it could possibly destroy its source, both spiritually and physically, and thus destroy itself. I would truly like to see both ministries survive under healthy, self-supporting principles of spiritual and physical growth. The Arkansas land payment must not be made by income dependent on my music ministry. I must give the land to someone interested in lay community who can pay for it from a legitimate source, or I must sell it altogether and forget about using it for community purposes. If it is to be used in the community vision, it must exist by healthy principles that are both scriptural and in keeping with Christian tradition.

September 9, 1978—6:00 P.M.— Greenville, S.C.

I see that I must rid myself of my van, my insurance, and my land if my ministry is to be truly free to function under scriptural and traditional principles. Jesus tells the apostles that their ministry is to go forth in a poverty that requires little yet gives much. He assures them that they will be taken care of, and in fact they were. This is due to God's providence and the practical fact that they needed very little to exist. The early church did the same thing. All extra-local ministers were forbidden to ask for any money in return for their ministries. They could do this only because they, like the apostles before them, went forth in a life of poverty that requires very little for existence. Likewise, I must now become truly poor so that my ministry will be dependent on very little. Then will my ministry be free to ride the wind of the Spirit without hindrance. Then will my ministry remain pure.

September 10, 1978—9:00 A.M.—Atlanta

Last night I had a very successful ministry in Greenville, and received only $60 over my expenses in return. I had asked the Lord to make my feelings and theories about poverty and my apostolate clear to me through an experience. I feel that last night was an answer to prayer. The ministry was very well received by a crowd of about 500 people, yet the Lord did not allow the offering to be as much as is usually received from a crowd of 50. I noticed an anxiety within me due to the small offering. But had my home expenses been less, the small offering would have made no difference. This leads me to believe that my anxiety is not rooted in the small offering, but rather is rooted in my large overhead. I am convinced that the scriptural and traditional admonition to apostolic poverty that never asks for financial reward is logically possible only because of the poor life-style of the apostolic minister. Once again, I must cut my overhead to an overhead of scriptural and traditional apostolic poverty so that my ministry will be built solidly on a strong foundation of gracious charity and Godly order. Then will my ministry truly prosper.

September 11, 1978—10:00 P.M.—Alverna

I must depart from the theme of disposing of possessions to relate the moving of the Spirit today. I have met some leaders of the charismatic renewal here in town. They are very excited about the Third Order as the possible answer to the move toward community within the charismatic renewal. They agree that it will provide order, unity, and an official affiliation with the guidance of the church for the various communities coming forth in all strata of the Indianapolis area in general. They also feel strong "leadings" toward Eureka Springs, Arkansas. This must be more than mere "coincidence."

We had much fellowship in the Lord's Spirit, and his movement toward gathering his people in community is apparent. I actually believe this Third Order community idea could be applied all over the world. The most obvious places I feel would be Indianapolis, Jerusalem, and Eureka Springs. I feel this is so simply because of the sympathetic contacts I have in all three of these places.

I also feel closer to discovering the Catholic structure from which to bring forth my ministry. I feel it should be a combination of charismatic renewal and Third Order in a new move toward community that I will now call simply "Charity." This means discussing my ministry with the leaders of both the Third Order and the charismatic renewal. Upon the release of my new album this will be easy, owing to the liturgical nature of my new music; but perhaps I might at least establish contacts with these leaders before the album release.

My ministry would be a combination of three basic thrusts. The first would obviously be music. This would involve major concerts and informal sharing sessions in a local area. The second would be seminars for local music ministers. In these I would discuss many of the points discussed in this journal, such as Christian contemporary rock music as it relates to Christian contemporary liturgy and ministry. I could also discuss the structural and financial aspects of both these ministries. The third thrust would include a basic sharing of the Third Order community vision as it relates to charismatic community. The importance of variety and an understanding tolerance of seemingly different community visions would be emphasized as the key to gathering all the communities in a healthy unity in the simple cross and the resurrection of Jesus. Of course, all of these ministries would be offered in an interdenominational outreach, but the Catholic base as the key to structural unity would never be side-stepped.

This has been a good day. Jesus allowed me to get sick so that I would slow down long enough to pray these things through. Now I simply rest in his arms as he nurses me back to health. I pray for a speedy recovery.

September 22, 1978—10:55 A.M.*—Toronto*

Great thinkers have often said that man lives most of his life in a quiet, subdued despair. He fills his world with complexities in order to provide relief and fulfillment but in the end he is always unable to escape this inner dread and solitude. I am convinced that Jesus does away with this solitary despair only by bringing meaning to it. Christian man cannot escape this despair and inner dread, for he too is human. He too often tries to fill his life with complex theories and complicated gadgets in order to escape this dread and bring a sense of purpose to his life. He is, like other people, extremely frightened by this inner silence and solitude that is with him always. But he, like others, cannot escape loneliness in his inner being by outer devices, and this eventually brings despair. When the day is done, when all the words of men are silent, when all the companions have retired to their own isolated beds, even when lovers have retired to the solitude of their own thoughts, then will the Christian, like other men, come face to face with the darkness of the night and the solitary silence of his own soul. In Christian charity we may rightly help fill many of the outer voids in one another's lives, but we cannot bear one another's burden of inner solitude and silence. We may feed the hungry and clothe the naked. We may love the unloved and befriend the friendless. We may guide the misdirected and counsel the uncounseled. But no man can bear the burden of another man's inner loneliness that prevails after the parting of companions. Only Jesus can bear this burden, for only he brings meaning to the burden of this darkness and this living death by the example of his passion. Because Jesus also has experienced the darkness and the death of the cross, we may now have constant fellowship with him in our own passion of inner dying and despair. The dying and the despair will still continue, but now they take on a passionate meaning that is eternal. In knowing Jesus through the cross, we now have hope in his resurrection through eternity. In this living death we surely find a new life of passion in dying with him.

I seek to rid myself of these outer complexities so I may come face-to-face with my inner despair and there find the cross of Jesus. Away with the endless gadgets and theories that occupy my mind in the name of "escape from boredom." Away with the endless conversations that are justified by the word "fellowship." Let me come face-to-face with my boredom with the silent cross of Jesus, so that I may rightly see my sin for what it is. Let me face my despair and loneliness in the dark night, so that I may repent and cry in passion to the Lord. Let me cry the tears that my inner self constantly cries, rather than fill my outer self with superficial laughter. Then will my life with Jesus be real. Then will I find the deeper worship of God that is found in spirit and truth.

Contemplative community is aimed at bringing a little brother or sister face-to-face with this reality The community life should not nurture superficial complexities; it should rid itself of them so as to bring its members into a life of spiritual reality in love and truth. Physical needs should be met in love, but physical complexities that only cloud the contemplative search for true reality should be done away with. The same holds true for community relationships. Relationships must never be an escape from this inner reality of the human condition and the cross of Jesus. They must rather grow from face-to-face confrontation with this reality, and they must only lead us back to this reality. Our community love relationships must grow from the confrontation with the cross in silence and solitude, and they must lead us back only to that same cross. Thus will the community as a whole know the beauty of the resurrection of Jesus in community life. So let there be a minimum of possessions and words in community; then shall we possess the wealth of the Lord's kingdom, and hear only the Living Word. Then shall our life take on a passionate meaning that makes initial boredom our door to true activity and the cross of Jesus our door to his resurrection.

October 1, 1978—Alverna

It seems as if my own real vocation is drawing very close. I find less and less to write about, for my inner experiences cannot be verbalized. I can say I feel my ministry coming to an end, and I feel a period of solitary contemplative prayer beginning. I desire only to be nothing. To be poor. To be silent. To be alone. To live a simple life of prayer, study, and work in my hermitage. To be free to wander when God so directs. To be free to live in prayer of solitude for long periods of time when God so directs. I seek to disappear so that only Jesus will be seen. Let the woods cover my house and the ivy cover my path. Let the sounds of the creek and the creatures cover the sound of my voice that so often speaks without praising God. Let me be satisfied with solitude. Let me be satisfied with silence. Then will the world feel my presence and hear my words. Then will the world see only Jesus as they search in vain for me.

October 9, 1978—10:00 P.M.—Alverna

My dad has nearly died several times since October 4th. His heart has failed. His lungs have failed. It is possible that his mind has failed as well. I cannot describe what I am experiencing. I feel as if I am dying so that he might be healed. I am downcast in hopes of his uplifting in Jesus. I feel as if I would take his sickness if only Jesus would heal him and bring him peace. In this I join with the sacrifice of Jesus. I pray that in this my father may be resurrected and healed.

October 16, 1978—10:00 A.M.*—Alverna*

I believe that God is telling me something this week. He is telling me this through my father's illness and through the "illness," or lack of power, in my ministry.

He has asked me to turn from the things of the world, and yet I refused. As this journal shows, I have rationalized his call to the point of annulling it. But God's call will not be annulled! We will obey his word of life or suffer the death of spiritual separation from him. God has asked me many times to follow him into poverty and solitude. Yet I have remained in affluence and influential action, all the time claiming to know this poverty and solitude. This is a lie and is sin! I should die in this sin if justice prevails; but in my case, I am not the one who is dying. My father is dying. My ministry too is dying. Yet in their death, I feel an equal death in the depths of my heart. I am convinced that all else that I refuse to leave behind will likewise die. Yes, my mother, my brother, and sister. All my possessions shall be taken from me if I do not give them willfully. All my rights shall be taken if I do not give them up on my own. Oh Lord, let me die now so my family might live! Accept the sacrifice of my life for theirs. In my poverty let them find wealth in you. In my foolishness, let them find wisdom in you. In my cross, let them find resurrection in you. Jesus, give me the strength to know the weakness of your death. Then will I know the power of your resurrection.

It is strange that a year ago today, both my wife and my child were taken from me. Perhaps God is simply continuing my death.

October 22, 1978—10:00 P.M.*—Alverna*

I need to reestablish a daily discipline in my life. I simply am trying to do too many things at once. The Mass, the hermitage, my father's affairs in his sickness, my apostolate, the community, and the disposal of my property. It is all beyond me! I long for the simplicity of an orderly routine so that I might persevere in study, work, and prayer. God help me in this work of contemplative living.

October 29, 1978—10:00 P.M.*—Alverna*

I am a pilgrim. I do not belong to this world. The world speaks of power, when love's power is in Christ's weakness. The world speaks of profit, when the profit of the cross is in loss. This is the only power and profit I know.

How can I exist in this world and still be a follower of Jesus' literal footsteps? Even to minister to this Western world with modern media, we must use vast amounts of money. And to use great amounts of money, we must deal in the ethics of profit. I cannot ever make an album without plotting the sale of the album! Can I just be an artist and liturgist? No! I must be a damned salesman as well! The ethics of Western man are so predominant that they even infiltrate the ethics of the religious communities that were originally established only to minister the ethics of the kingdom of heaven. Even if I don't personally deal in the profit ethic of capitalistic success, the man who donates his "tax write-off" must. How can a Christian called literally to the selfless mercy of the cross prosper in a world that deals in self-centered justice at best? Not that justice is bad, but selfless mercy is better. Surely it is a true miracle of God when a businessman or contemporary minister prospers in this world when he really exists under the ethics of the kingdom of heaven.

Dear Jesus, let me truly die to anything of this world, so I too might taste of heaven. Then if you will that I might prosper in a large ministry, so be it. But only then. Let me be a lily of the field. If I am transplanted to the city, then so be it. A windowbox. A crack in the pavement. Wherever. There will I grow. But as a lily I will not seek to become the pavement or the concrete and steel that surround me in order to control or reach my environment . . . I must be only a lily. Willing to live in the field or the city, yet willing to die when there are no fields left or no cracks left in the city streets. Willing to be lifted up to the tallest skyscraper, yet willing to be torn up by the roots by a demolition crew. At the mercy of man. At the mercy of God. This is the call of the lily of the field. To die is nothing, for we are dead already in the cross. Fear is gone. Pain is gone. Life is gone. All we experience now is grace.

All life is grace . . . both good and bad. All our time lived is now a resurrection. Therefore, to die in the flesh means only to live in the spirit. To be crowded out by the concrete in death is simply to go on to a place where fields are eternally beautiful to behold and fragrant to smell. These fields are truly eternal! They cannot be taken from us! These fields await all lilies who carry on as pilgrims and beggars in the city of this world. This is our lot in this concrete world. This is our assurance and hope in the fields of heaven. This is our cause for true rejoicing and comfort. This is our true ministry to a world of despair!

Flowers bring life to a dead world of concrete and steel.

November 2, 1978—11:00 P.M.*—Alverna*

Tonight I consider several things. I am acutely aware of my inner solitude. No matter how many loving Christians accompany me, I am still in interior solitude. There is really very little even my closest brothers and sisters can share of my interior loneliness. Only Jesus can really accompany me on my pilgrimage, but even he seems far away. Yet in this loneliness, I have fellowship with him who once was also alone on a cross, separated even from his Father in heaven. Thus even in my seeming separation from Jesus, I am closer to him than I have ever been before. I actually begin to share in his interior suffering. I experience the passion of his agony. I experience his darkest night. In this I have fellowship in his light and the comfort of his resurrected life in my dying self.

I can see that many of my "Christian" relationships are really not centered on the real Jesus. These relationships may resound with doctrinally correct conversations or even expositions on the love of Christ and the contemplative life. Yet few of these relationships bring us to and nurture that inner solitude that is necessary if we are really to know the interior companionship of love of Christ. We must all realize the validity of this inner solitude, and learn to edify one another by allowing one another this grace. We must simply let one another "be," even as Jesus simply "IS." No more pretentious conversations. No more idle talk. Let us seek simply to "be" in humility and love. In this we would do well.

November 5, 1978—2:30 P.M.*—Alverna*

I went to see my little girl this weekend. I am amazed how she has grown. She is both loving and bright. I am proud of her. I am aware of God's grace in her little life. Even though the family is constantly changing as people within it struggle and grow, Amy is still growing with seeming ease. Even though the family tree seems irrevocably twisted in a complex knot, Amy's little branch seems to be growing straight and sure. Her branch is very tender, but this just might be the strength that has kept her from snapping in half. I am aware that in my present absence, God is with her. I can now give her love, but I am really no longer her father in the sense of giving her daily support and guidance. The Father must now care for her. I love her more now than I ever have before, yet I see that I must substantially detach myself from the entire family if Amy is to grow without the further confusion of seemingly having "two daddies." This is hard now, but it will make it easier for her. I will see her but only occasionally so that my love for her cannot be erased from her memory. My prayers and occasional embraces will have to do. God must do the rest.

November 8, 1978—12:30 A.M.—Alverna

I have sewn the habit of the vision this past day. It is made of second-hand army blankets I acquired from an army surplus store. I must say that I feel very comfortable in it, even though it is alien to all my cultural conditioning, and I am sure this is the habit of the vision. I now seek only the blessing of the provincial and the Alverna community.

In seeking this blessing, I am aware of my own doubts about God's call. I seek only to obey the vision of faith, but my mind keeps telling me how silly it is to be concerned about a habit. Granted, it is silly to be anxious about clothing, but this clothing is sacramental because it was fashioned by Jesus! Therefore, my seeking the habit is not just seeking clothing, but is a seeking to obey God's call. This is not overanxious materialism. This is simply a desire to obey the Spirit of God! Nonetheless, I have tried every way out. I have spiritualized the vision. I have rationalized the vision. I have even changed the design of the habit better to suit today's world. I have done everything but obey. So today I must obey, and obey I will.

The habit is different from those worn by other Orders. It is coarse and brownish-green in color. It is open at the throat with a hood attached to the collar. Both the throat opening and the hood tie with leather thread. If I use a cord, it will be of old rope, or if the provincial approves, I will use the traditional Franciscan cord. Most of all, it is patched and worn. It is a symbol of my royal poverty in Jesus. It is a symbol of my consecration unto him. It is a constant reminder of both of these as long as I wear it.

Again, I am not claiming any special spirituality by taking this habit. I am not claiming to be a friar when I am unworthy to be so called. I am not attempting to copy Francis in some kind of make-believe drama. I simply seek to be who I am and to follow God's call for me in childlike simplicity. I hope that in taking this habit I am doing only this.

December 20, 1978—Evening—Hermitage

Well, it has begun. The hermitage is built, the habit is made, and they have both been blessed by God and by Father Martin. We had a lovely dedication Mass down here several days ago. I felt the special presence of God. It was good.

I have also played my last concert for quite some time. I cannot describe how good it feels to get away from the materialistic and negative gossip that goes on in the Christian contemporary music ministry. I look forward to working from an ecumenical Catholic base that is well-balanced and tested with time.

My father is very sick, and sometimes I think he cannot possibly live much longer. Never have I seen such good will in a man so ill. I have truly learned to love and respect my dad in a way words can't describe. I pray that the Lord heals him quickly, for he cannot stand much more of this torment. I wish I could suffer so that he could be comforted.

I have never been through so many changes in so short a time. It is as if I am dying too, and my former life is playing before me like a movie. I truly appreciate the good times I have had. But I am also learning I cannot go back. I cannot be born again until I die. I cannot fly with the wind-dancing grace of the butterfly until I hide away in the loneliness of my cocoon. I feel alone. I feel helpless. I feel useless to the world. Yet I know I must flee the world and all it holds if I am to learn how to serve it as God wills. I am afraid, yet I am sure. I am learning to love, yet some think I have grown cold by withdrawing. I am also learning to cry. It is dark here, yet dawn brings a new light.

Sometimes I think I have surely lost my mind. These feelings are really quite irrational for a Christian American boy. Sometimes I think I must be demon-possessed, yet Christ's deliverance always draws me closer to the cross. The cross! Oh God, let this cup pass from me! I do not want to die! But death is the only way out of living in a dying world. Let death come, Lord Jesus. Let me know your pain and your suffering. Let me know the humiliation and rejection you knew. Let me know your loneliness and your tears. Let me know the passion of dying so I might know the joy of life again. Let my flesh be torn and let my heart burst. Let me offer myself to you as a sacrifice for your church and your world. Let me share in the work you have completed on Calvary.

Let me love you, Lord Jesus. This alone do I now seek.

Sunday, December 24, 1978—11:00 A.M.— Hermitage

A cold start this morning. Even the paper refused to burn. But, "let patience have its perfect work," a nice fire is now burning and the room is slowly warming. I feel much better these last two days. A joy that comes from assuredness has come back to me. I am sure of my calling. However, I do still feel the need to "belong." I do so wish there was a religious Order that was "right" for me. Of course, there is the entire church. You would think that would be community enough! But I still feel the need for direct support, even in solitude and silence. I still feel a close affinity with both the Little Brothers of St. Francis and the Camaldolese. I wonder if I am not called to a little of both. A structure like the Little Brothers (as Third Order Secular, yet vowed) and a discipline like the Camaldolese excepting that younger men could embark on limited apostolates for short periods of time. Well, whatever. I am secure in my own call, but I still seek the guidance of some brothers. Funny, I will probably seek my vocation until the day I die.

It just started snowing. Hallelujah! We just might have a white Christmas. I also almost burned my tunic. I laid it over the stove to warm it and suddenly smelled a very peculiar odor. Oh well, I have patches for it.

It occurs to me that the main difference between my calling and that of the Camaldolese is the freedom I think the younger men should have to embark on a mendicant-like apostolate for limited times. The Camaldolese may do this only at an older age after successfully living a life of solitude and silence. I agree this time is needed for the young men if their apostolates are to be rich in God's wisdom, but I do think that, if their spiritual directors agree, they should be allowed a limited apostolate if they are truly called of God to this. So I emphasize the discipline of solitary prayer, but I also allow freedom for an apostolate among people.

December 25, 1978—5:30 P.M.*—Hermitage*

A good Christmas! Spent the day with my parents and brother and sister. I do love them all. However, my separation in solitude is evident and I hope it won't confuse them. I pray that they will understand that my solitude is as much for them as it is for me.

I read Thomas Merton on "the hermitage" in *Monastic Journey*. His proposed discipline struck me as very good. I lack discipline, so I see its need. However, I do see the need for freedom as well. This mendicant flavor will not leave the taste buds of my vocation. Benedict, forgive me! St. Francis, bless me! Time in the hermitage should be disciplined, but time in the world should be allowed so the freedom of solitude may be shared. What a paradox! You cannot tell people of silence with words, yet the only way to share solitary silence is by words. Paradox!

December 26, 1978—1:45 P.M.—Hermitage

A good day so far. Chopped some wood, wrote a song prayer around Psalm 62, and studied some more Merton on solitude (what else?). A good fire going now, so I think I will read some scripture, if I don't get too bored. (Has been known to happen!)

December 26, 1978—10:00 P.M.—Hermitage

Some friends dropped by and asked me over to eat dinner with them and their one-and-one-half-year-old daughter. I accepted with hesitation, but did not want to offend by saying no. Had a lovely evening, but not much was communicated. I sensed something wrong there, but cannot say exactly what. Nonetheless, they are dear friends and I love them very much.

Through this, I am convinced that my solitude should be disciplined if it is to work. Then will I serve both God and my neighbor more in accordance with God's will for me and them. Perhaps my solitude and my silent example will communicate more than my words and my visits. Perhaps the paradox should stop there. The word of God that comes in silence is best communicated when left unsaid. I hope my friends can learn this despite my undisciplined example. Perhaps this unspoken word of love could fill the gap that so obviously torments them subconsciously. My friends, I lay down my life for you in Jesus. May you live in my dying, just as I now live in the dying of Christ.

December 27, 1978—6:30 P.M.—Hermitage

A good warm day. The sun shone brightly outside and the fire blazed continually inside. Spent early hours chopping wood and then studied a book called *Mary in the New Testament*. It is a very "Protestant" book, written by Catholic scholars. Quite frankly, most of it is beyond me. I am getting a lot from it nonetheless. My love for Mary is increasing in proportion to my knowledge of her in church development. But my love for her remains simple.

Two workers from Alverna dropped in and chopped quite a lot of wood for me this afternoon. I was amazed at how quickly their chain saw cuts wood. They cut in five minutes what normally would have taken me more than one hour. The noise, though, does disturb the calm of these woods. I can't decide between a few minutes of noise or a few hours of tiring sawing. But what if everybody had chain saws? Then the noise would be as constant as the sound of the trucks and cars on the freeway. God forbid! Limit their use, or chop by hand. Then will these peaceful woods remain a grace from a peaceful God.

I concluded the day by sitting against an immense old tree on a hill and watching the sun set. I watched the creek. I watched the woodsmoke dance from my hermitage chimney and fill the valley with a "good-smelling" pollution. All in all I was at peace within myself. I thanked God for the gift of living today and for receiving new eyes in Jesus to see his blessings in creation. It was a good day.

December 28, 1978—9:00 A.M.*—Hermitage*

I rose a little later than usual owing to the cold in the room. The fire went out about 2:00 A.M.; so I retreated under my covers to find warmth. By the time I woke up I hesitated to stick my toe onto the cold floor because of the frozen condition of my iced nose. I knew it would be cold outside, and I was very warm and snug inside. So, I prayed some "under cover."

I finally rose about 7:30 and started a fire. It started slowly, but is now burning with a slow, warm flame. Because my wood supply was low, I was forced to spend about forty-five minutes chopping wood before prayers and meditation. After accumulating a nice pile, I said morning prayers and spent some time reading and in reflection. Because of my eventual trip to the airport today, I am having a hard time settling down to real stillness. I keep thinking of the things I must do today. Oh well, at least I had close to an hour of good prayer time today. Lord Jesus, send me your inner peace with which to face this busy day. Let me love everyone I meet, even the airport police. Amen.

December 28, 1978—10:00 P.M.—Hermitage

Back from my activities. Picked up Cheri White, my concert coordinator at the airport, lined up my engagements for spring, and went to the studio. Talked for about two hours with Cheri about the Catholic Church and the contemplative life. It was good. I think one such active day a week is good for me. It keeps me in touch with the people Jesus loves. But this day must be disciplined, or else eventually my solitude will no longer exist, and then my ministry to those people will be less effective.

December 29, 1978—3:00 P.M.—Hermitage

Just rose from a half-hour nap. Outside, all the woods have come alive. The ice from the freezing rain this morning is melting and big drops of water are falling from all the trees. It is creating quite a stir. The birds were all singing, and the squirrels are all out running. It was a good scene to wake up to.

Earlier, I rose about 7:30 A.M. I couldn't cut much wood due to the freezing rain, so I wrote the liner notes for the next album. I also worked on a new musical Mass. It is more complex than this last one and totally different in feel. It is more abstract, yet much more structured due to performing the abstraction correctly. I then ventured back to the woods to gather wood. I returned to my cell and sang some more. After that I was very tired. Singing and composing always tires me more than anything else. I then decided to take the nap I just described above.

I cannot describe the peace I feel. I truly feel as if I have come "home." Now I can simply "be." Oh, I still fight many temptations to leave my vocation, but all contemplatives have fought this same fight, so why waste paper? What I am saying is this: it is good simply to become one with these woods. It is good to be able to experience God's blessing in them. I feel as if I am beginning to settle in and getting to "serious business." No more philosophizing about solitude and silence. I am now beginning to *live* solitude and silence. My thoughts have begun to change. They are now very simple and childlike. I am concerned only with the woods and my fire. I am really enjoying life! I am grateful to God for his many graces. I thank him for allowing me to hold just some of them.

December 30, 1978—11:00 A.M. *—Hermitage*

Couldn't sleep last night. I stayed up writing and praying until about midnight. I rose this morning about five and stayed in prayer until seven. It was raining all that time, so I went back to sleep. I rose again about nine and went up the hill to shower. I am seriously considering cutting my hair army style to avoid the hassle when it gets dirty. That would also clear up my scalp condition. Not that I wouldn't bathe, but I wouldn't feel so grungy before I bathe. Said mid-morning office up the hill with Cheri, and gave her some letters to type. I am grateful for her charitable spirit.

Since coming back down the hill, I have cleaned my cell. It was really dirty from mud, wood dust, and ashes. It looks a little better now. I also gathered more wood. I then spent some time in prayer

and reflection by the creek. Jesus taught me a neat lesson while re-
flecting on the movement of the water. This is the lesson:

A creek is made up of both calm and rapids. Most of the water is
calm except when there is an obstacle in the way. Then the water
moves with quickness and obvious power. The power is in the
calm, but it is less obvious and more kinetic. It is the obstacle that
causes the great power of the water to be made manifest. The calm
area is easily navigated by small boats and canoes. They may go,
at will, from shore to shore without resistance. But in the rapids,
the boat must follow the flow of the water. It has very little control
over its own navigation. If it fights the flow of the water's power,
it usually ends up crashing into the obstacle that is causing the
rapids in the first place.

The creek is like a contemplative. The boat is like an active
man. The obstacle is religious opposition. The calm area repre-
sents the contemplative time of prayer and solitude. The rapids
represent the time of active apostolates.

Eventually, the obstacle is moved by the power of the creek. But
the creek must be calm most of the time if the rapids are to be truly
strong. Most of the boats make their way safely through the rapids
if they follow the course of the creek. Only those who oppose the
creek end up with the same fate as the obstacle. Eventually, all obstacles line the creek and serve it by making the shore well defined.
In the end, all the water, and most of the boats, find their way to
the great sea.

For me, this means I must spend most of my time in solitary
prayer. I must be calm and passive during these times. Then, quite
naturally, my short times of ministry will be powerful and strong.
My apostolate will then move obstacles and make it safe for all
people to use me to reach union with Jesus, who is the Great Sea
toward whom all God's people flow.

After learning this lesson, I went back to my cell. After I stoked
the fire, Brother Paul came in. He brought me some bread and
checked out a leak in my wall. He then reproved me for making
my footpath wrong. He said it could cause erosion in the hill. He

again exhorted me to slow down in my work and do things right. I know he is right, and I will try to do better. I love Paul very much. He has been a strong support to me in my vocational search. I hope he loves me too under all that fatherly sternness.

December 30, 1978—2:00 P.M.—Hermitage

They just started on the trees up the hill with *two* chain saws. The amount of wood cut is amazing, but I must say that it is nearly impossible to hear the "little things" of the woods with all that powerful racket. I do envy them with all that wood, but the noise is almost extreme. Of course, this could be considered "natural." Man, as he is, is part of the planned environment. It is also quite a commotion when a cat kills its prey. The woods seem quite dangerous then. I suppose man is just hunting his "prey" . . . a dead tree up the hill. I do look forward to the promised day when the lion will lie down with the lamb. Lord Jesus, restore your original peace and rest to mankind and all creation. I believe you will do this some day . . . maybe even soon. Maranatha!

It just started to pour down rain from heaven. They had to stop cutting wood with those saws! Praise God for rain from heaven. However, due to my envy, it is now impossible for me to share in their spoils. I cannot even go out and cut my own. Ah . . . God is merciful and kind . . . but he is also just.

December 30, 1978—3:30 P.M.—Hermitage

I just walked and prayed by the creek. It was raining. I learned another lesson. The stream always changes. There is not one day, or even one hour, when the stream doesn't change. Sometimes it looks cold, other times it looks like a tropical swamp. I mean the "look" of the water. Not the color or the clearness. I mean the actual texture of the water. It is as we should be. Ever constant . . . ever changing.

The currents change as well. The creek bed also constantly changes. The shoreline is in a constant state of change. It is amazing how we think of it always the same, when it is never the same. Only its power and its presence are constant. Again, we should be like the creek. The love and the presence of Jesus should remain constant in our lives, yet the specifics of how we apply his love each day should always be open to change. This is the way of the creation of God. It should be the way of God's people as well. Then will we overcome the obstacles in our life, just as the stream eventually overcomes its obstacles as well.

The creek has taught me much. Contemplation? Yes. Apostolate? Yes. Discipline and definition? Yes. But freedom to grow day by day as well! To flow with the unforeseen circumstances and emergencies of life with human beings in a human world. This is a must if our contemplation is to be a natural living outgrowth of the living Spirit of Jesus.

December 30, 1978—7:00 P.M.—Hermitage

Had some unexpected visitors. My mom and dad dropped by. Dad looks much better. It was good to see him up and around.

Went to community Mass and then ate with the friars. It was good to "hang out" with them, worship with them, and relax with the joking of friends. However, this too must be disciplined. If I were to do this everyday, my solitude would be unreal, and they would lose respect for my vocation. Freedom? Yes. But discipline as well.

On the way back down the hill, I noticed a thick fog had settled about the creek. I walked into the cloud to find my cell. Soon the big house of the friars was lost from my sight. Nor could I see my

91

cell in the fog-covered woods. I then realized that my family and the wondering about a vocational call to the friars was behind me. The future yet before me. I have entered into the great cloud of God's mystery. The cloud of forgetting, the cloud of unknowing, the cloud in which all true contemplatives must eventually disappear. Then will they be truly found by the Savior of all lost children. I now seek to live within this great cloud of God's paschal mystery . . . the cloud of unknowing. Amen. Let me be a little child, Lord Jesus, then shall I be wiser than the greatest scholar.

January 1, 1979—6:30 P.M.*—Hermitage*

Happy New Year! This is the feast of Mary, the mother of God. An eventful day, full of work, prayer, and temptations. I should have known it would be such a day when I rose at 3:00 A.M. and prayed for two solid hours, totally losing track of time. The prayer time was rich, but the day that followed could not have been endured without such prayer.

First, upon reaching the end of my prayers, it started to rain. This would make two and one-half days of solid rain and sleet. Later the rain turned to hail, and then to snow. Eventually everything in the wooded hills was soaked. The hill was mud, and the once burnable wood was soaked with unburnable water. Later the temperature dropped and helped at least make the footing a little more solid.

Next I went out to try and find some dry wood. There was very little to be found. I pulled down a dead limb that had fallen into the "V" of a living tree and got some fairly usable stuff. Next I sawed down a dead tree by the creek. This took about forty-five minutes. But after going back up the hill to get the axe, things went quickly. Soon I had a good-size pile of frozen, but dry, wood. However, once I brought the wood to the warm indoors, the frozen part melted and became . . . "water." This water dripped through the pile and got most of the wood quite wet. It also got the floor of my cell quite wet. But trials have their reward. This somewhat wet wood seems to be burning nicely for it burns with heat, but it burns slowly.

I then began studying the "scholarly" book *Mary in the New Testament*. I have described this book once before. Today, however, all those scholarly guesses about origins really got me down. These guys seem to tear apart all the basics of Christianity with speculation and then come back with, "But none of this can be proven one way or the other." These men have solid faith in solid truth, but sometimes their theories are vain for the spirit. I would rather just "trust in the Lord with all my heart and lean not to my own understanding." My faith comes from a relationship of heartfelt love with Jesus, not from an intellectual speculation about the outer qualities of Jesus. However, through all their theories, they are getting back to the original church's understanding of Mary and the reason for her blessed place in hearts and history. This reason is simply her humility and obedience. She should not be placed as high as many Catholics often place her. She is not God! Even though theology and church doctrine never said she was, the laymen and women of the church misplaced their worship of Jesus with worship of Mary. This is an error in the faith. But she is a beautifully obedient and humble woman who was graced with bearing Jesus the Lord in her womb because of both God's grace and her obedient response of true faith to that grace. However, it must be kept in mind by the laymen that even her obedience is a gift from our gracious Lord. Oh well, sweet Mary, mother of God, may God be praised through your life, and may we, your brothers, sisters, sons, and daughters, be remembered in your prayers to Jesus, who is the Savior of us all!

Anyway, through all this scholarly humanism I began to have some serious doubts myself. Again, this is my weakness, not an error on the part of the book. I soon began to question if even the apostles and the first church were anywhere close. Perhaps they just blew it. Maybe Jesus never objectively promised the Holy

Spirit to guide his Church infallibly to all objective truth. Maybe the objective truth about Jesus, Mary, and all the rest simply cannot be had anymore. Maybe things are just too obscured by heresy and erroneous tradition. Even if this is true (which I still don't think is the case), the existential and contemplative side to Christianity opens one's inner soul to the highest heights of even the most advanced alternative . . . Eastern religion. The paradox of the cross out-mystifies any of the other religions' mystics. So, even if the objective truth of Christianity is all wrong about Jesus, my faith in him has still advanced beyond the existential truths of other alternative religions. I cannot lose my faith. I am justified by the East . . . and I am justified by the West.

But it is both the objective and the subjective truths of the faith that have caused me to become a Catholic. In the Roman Catholic Church I perceive the authority, through a unified apostolic college and succession, to establish a unity of doctrine of objective truth. This leaves the serious contemplative free to go on to the mystical heart of a relationship with Jesus without having constantly to check the objective truth of the relationship in order to make sure they are really living Jesus. Thus, the Catholic contemplative can venture into the depths of the existential God without having to worry constantly about the objective identity of God. He can deal exclusively with the unexplainable heart of our Lord that is far beyond words. He can deal with the pure light of love in absolute trust in the identity of the Lover who is the Giver of pure Light.

I cannot return to my former strict fundamentalist thinking. This thinking placed absolute authority in the Bible, totally writing off tradition as "perversion of the Word." As a Catholic, I also place the highest authority in the Bible, but authoritatively interpreted in light of early church tradition. This is simply done because the oral and written traditions of the early church produced the written Word; therefore, the written Word can only be properly interpreted by going back to examine the witness of the early church Fathers in order to establish what those traditions were. This is easily done, even by the laymen, thanks to English translations of almost all these works. Consequently, a Catholic too has a zeal for the Word. But that Word is not limited to a black-and-white page that never grows or breathes. That Word is a living Word. It has lived in the living people of God from the beginning. That Word breathes. It is not a black-and-white text. That Word is a living Jesus! Nor is it solely interpreted by private individuals who set up their own separate churches, but rather by an authority traceable to Jesus and the apostles in scripture and tradition through apostolic succession.

If there were no Roman Catholic Church, there would be no scripture upon which my Protestant brethren so zealously base their sincere faith. If there is no objective truth to the Roman Catholic Church which compiled and first interpreted the scriptures, then there can be no attainable objective truth for Christians. Then we might as well be Zen Buddhists.

But, more importantly, I have found the Roman Catholic Church to be the surest vehicle by which the Christian contemplative can soar beyond even the highest heights of the Zen Master. The cross . . . the cross . . . oh beautiful paradox of love . . . centrality of our faith and worship! I adore the Jesus of the simple cross. I share my life and love with him in my constant dying. May I also share now in his resurrection.

Anyway, it is late. I can see that a night with a fire and wet wood has begun. I'd better bundle up, for it is cold outside. I feel better after having written. My faith is restored once again. Hallelujah!

January 1, 1979—9:00 P.M.—Hermitage

Couldn't sleep. Had to write more on this subject before I could shut my eyes and also shut my brain for the night.

From the contemplative view of existential love in Jesus, my heart longs for a reuniting of all the people of the Christian faith.

Jesus said that if we weren't united in love, then the world would not believe that he was and is real. I believe that the eschatological regathering of Israel, foretold by the prophets as a sign of the end times, is a type to symbolize the regathering of the dispersed church back into her original homeland. I believe we will be reunited *before* Jesus returns.

Meanwhile, we must try and heal the cracks of division that come from the plethora of personal interpretations of Scripture and personal claims to authority, either prophetic or apostolic. Granted, a true prophet may claim existential, personal authority from God. But God's church has been built upon apostles, not prophets. The prophets must continue to exhort and edify that church through prophecy coming from the wilderness, but the authority of an undivided church structure rests with the manifest apostolic office passed on from the beginning by the apostles themselves. The prophets still cry out to good effect in the wilderness of that structure, similar to the "school of prophets" in the Old Testament. Today, many of them can be found in the contemplative religious orders.

Division leads to chaos, and chaos is not of God, for in chaos there can be no unity, and without unity there can be no manifestation of love. Without a unity of true love, the world will not believe in the real Jesus.

From an existential desire for unity among Christians, I must look to the authority of the church in order to bring that unity to pass in a way that is consistent with the scripture, with philosophy, and with the early church witness of history.

Oh well, I must get some sleep. The sun is up and I have slept only a few hours. Looking over my notes, I must emphasize the simplification of this whole discussion. Of course, there are so many complex issues that surround all of this. There are so many Christians of all denominations who are both intelligent and devoted to the real Jesus. They experience God's grace as individuals to the fullest measure in the real Jesus. I do not want to belittle anyone's truly great faith. However, as long as we remain divided from one another, the full grace of God's salvation kingdom on earth will not be realized. Partial manifestation of this grace will be realized as we obtain partial unity. But God's full salvation for man will be realized only when unity has been restored under the original plan of Jesus.

January 2, 1979—11:00 A.M.*—Hermitage*

I was sitting next to a flowing stream this morning and, un-bidden, a thought about the development of dogma came to mind. A strange juxtaposition perhaps, but is not the development of church teaching much like that stream which runs smoothly and clearly until it reaches an obstacle? Then the water runs swiftly again, making itself obvious by its change of appearance and commotion. Now the water was always at-one-ment with the stream, but it was never made obvious to all until it met with the opposition of a rock, or a group of rocks, in its way.

Dogma is the same. It is not usually clarified by the church until someone, or some group, challenges its existence. By this threat to unity, the church is sometimes forced to fully define what she has always held to be integral to the whole. This is the way the Scriptures were first canonized for all Christians, and it is the way all major dogmas of the faith have been defined for Catholics and Protestants alike. It is certainly the way many of the doctrines peculiar to the Catholic Church were first clarified or defined. The stream of dogma is constantly changing as many similar but different obstacles are placed in its path; therefore, much of the same water of truth is manifested in different ways as it meets different challenges.

This means that as time flows forward from age to age, the church faces many new issues. Some of these issues were not met by the early apostolic church because there was no challenge, no obstacle. So in order to meet the issue, the church defines a dogma built with, and consistent with, the materials constructed by the early church. To compare the building of dogma to the stream helps me to see why certain Catholic beliefs took on a more sophisticated shape than were manifested by the early church. The stream and the water are one. There is no contradiction.

January 4, 1979—6:30 P.M.*—Hermitage*

Cold, cold, cold! Snow and more snow. I have chopped a lot of wood in this cold. I am tempted to buy a "noisy" chain saw, but I just don't know. I think Brother Paul would be upset by my inconsistency. I already have resorted to using coal to get me through the sub-zero nights.

Yesterday was my visiting day off the property. I went to see my parents and to do some paperwork concerning my music apostolate. It was good to get out, but I was glad to get back to my hermitage.

Today, however, somebody came to me for counseling and prayer. We talked and prayed for more than four hours. He thought he was demon-possessed. However, seeing his Spirit-given faith and desire in his life to know Jesus and his Spirit even more, it simply was not possible. God's Spirit and light casts out all devils of darkness from the possession of a man's soul. This man would not accept the grace of the Spirit because he was so sure he was possessed. Finally, I convinced him that the only thing the devil *was* doing was telling him a lie by telling him he was possessed. Once he realized this, he freely accepted God's grace of the Spirit in his life. It was a long, tiring experience. Praise Jesus. He has set the captive of deception free by speaking the truth of forgiveness and love. Hallelujah!

Tonight I feel very Franciscan. If I hadn't the freedom to spend most of my day with this man in need, I would not have fulfilled the gospel's admonition to give the gift I have received as a gift . . . to cast out devils . . . to love mankind with the love of Jesus. So today I broke my monastic discipline, but a soul was saved through prayer. This is the freedom of the first monks. This is the freedom of St. Francis!

January 6, 1979—9:00 P.M.*—Hermitage*

People have been coming to my cell door for two straight days. I cannot turn them away, for Jesus could not turn them away. So, again, my discipline is shot!

Still, got a lot of chopping done. Also a lot of praying. It was beautiful out chopping wood in a forest that was covered with fresh snow. All was still. All was silent. All was contemplating the restful calm of winter and the coming of spring.

Talked to Cheri White about the church tonight. We talked for over three hours. I almost got depressed for dwelling so much on objective truth when this woman desires only contemplative simplicity. If she becomes a Roman Catholic, it will probably be due to the Catholic freedom for contemplation, while still balancing that contemplative freedom with objective structure. She sees the need for objective structure to balance contemplative freedom, but will probably join the objective structure only so that her contemplative freedom may be secure from danger. Oh well, I hope I don't weigh down this little bird with too much dogma, so that it can't fly free in the wind. But the dogma is needed so the little bird can find her own flight path to heaven.

I feel contemplative again. Activity has been good, but now it is time to pray. I feel incapable of being a good spiritual leader. I am a sinner, far too unholy. I am in chains and cannot fly. How can I teach those with me how to fly, much less free them from captivity? Free me, sweet Jesus, let me fly with you to the heavens.

January 15, 1979—10:00 P.M.—Hermitage

Hurt my ankle and had to go up the hill. Just woke up a week ago and couldn't walk very well. I ended up on crutches all last week.

It turned out to be a week of emergency activities anyway. I had a real crisis with my album owing to a lack of understanding between myself and the people helping me. Again I came to realize my lack of leadership capabilities. I am either too lenient or too authoritative. I must learn to love with authority in a leadership capacity. I pray the Lord Jesus forgives me for this sin, for it has caused a lot of confusion.

I am thinking about taking private religious vows. Public vows are not right for me yet, for I do not belong to a religious community, nor do I feel worthy to start one. I thank the Lord that he is allowing me to make a vow again. I once took the Nazarite vow and broke it after seven years. God is giving me a gift with a second chance to be faithful. He is good.

I am considering the vows of apostolic poverty, contemplative prayer, and penance. Apostolic poverty fulfills the Lord's call to a part-time apostolate of poverty. Prayer fulfills the Lord's call to contemplation in substantial solitude and silence. Penance will be to remind me constantly of my sin in breaking the Nazarite vow, and it will remind me to be faithful to my vows this time in penance. I will vow to wear the holy habit of my vision in place of the divinely consecrated hair I once cut for human reasons. I might also vow obedience to Father Martin and the Alverna community, as well as taking the traditional vow of chastity. I would like to do this as soon as possible.

February 3, 1979—11:30 P.M.—Jerusalem

I have been thinking vocationally again. Thinking of the difference between my ministry here in Israel and in the States. In the States, I serve as an example of nonmaterialism and contemplation to those who are basically well-off, yet lack contemplative depth in Jesus. Here in Israel, the compactness of the city structure, especially in Jerusalem, brings real poverty right to the very doorstep of the rich. In the States the poor and the rich are separated by miles of "safety." The poor fill the walls of the Old City, and many beg alms at the city gates. Therefore, my ministry here in Jerusalem, if I ever should live here, would be similar to the ministry in the States concerning nonmaterialism and contemplation, but owing to the closeness of poverty, a more direct approach may be taken concerning the poor.

Around Jerusalem and Bethlehem many abandoned caves are available for use by religious hermits. In Jerusalem or Bethlehem I would try to live in one of these caves. Then I would nurture the contemplative side of my vocation. My apostolate would include singing for the local body of believers when they asked me to. I could also sing for the pilgrims when possible. But I would also sing as a begging troubadour for the Lord at the city gates. All the alms I collected from my apostolate would be distributed among those who are poor, not by religious choice, but by secular circumstances.

In the States, this is very difficult because of the geographical barrier between the poor and the rich. My life of apostolic poverty and solitary contemplation is fulfilled in the hermitage and in my singing apostolate. But in the States it is nearly impossible to walk from my hermitage in the woods to the poor in the inner city. And even in the inner city, there are few, if any, beggars. In order to "commute" from my hermitage to the poor, I would have to own a car or rent an apartment in the inner city to serve as a new hermitage. Thus my call to total poverty would not be fulfilled. The apostolate to the poor would not be as open as in Jerusalem. Singing in the welfare lines gets you thrown out of the welfare office. Only occasional street ministries would work for a troubadour. So, my financial ministry in the States would be suppoting the House of Prayer with my alms, so that the poor could also enjoy spiritual retreat, plus donating to worthy existing charities. This would allow me to keep my call to the hermitage intact, while also allowing for an apostolate of poverty as a troubadour for Jesus.

In both Jerusalem and the States I would be only a catalyst. The life God has called me to is not the ordinary Christian life, or the active agent. I serve only as a reminder, or a road sign to the promised land of the simplicity of the gospel life. But I am not worthy to cross over into the promised land. I am not an example of the normal Christian life in the land of promise. My sins are much too great. I must remain on Mount Nebo, only seeing others enter into the promise. I am but leaven, but the laity of the Body of Christ must be the actual bread that feeds the poor. I do not know why this is so. I only know that this is my call. I pray that Jesus graces me with loving presence so that I might persevere.

March 29, 1979—2:00 P.M.—Flight from Indianapolis to Akron

This is my first entry in over seven weeks. Most of this time I spent on a religious pilgrimage to the Holy Land. Owing to the interior changes wrought within me because of the trip, I have been unable to keep a journal. It is only now that I am beginning to be able to verbalize and define what has happened to me.

The two letters I sent home from Israel correctly relate my immediate impressions, with the exception of an overly negative tone related in the second letter. Overall, I learned that holiness is largely in the eye of the beholder. Both an intense holiness and unholiness are to be found in Israel. It is not unlike the rest of the world, except that, for some reason, it is much more intense concerning religious matters. I made many good friends there. I can only hope I ministered to them as much as they ministered to me. I do so pray for the interior peace of all Christians in Jerusalem and all of Israel, so that they may share this lasting inner peace of love with a people that are inwardly and outwardly torn by the confusion of hatred. May Jesus aid them to this end. Amen.

Upon my arrival back home, I began to realize just how disorienting the whole experience of Israel is to the Christian. I truly felt as if I had come home from intense combat. My mind and body were both drained of all strength. I must also say that even my spirit was on the brink of fatal exhaustion. People expected me to be strong and inspired in faith and hope, but in reality I was on the verge of doubt and despair. They expected me to have tasted the glory of the ascension on the Mount of Olives, but all I could tell them of was Jesus' tears over Jerusalem at Dominus Flavit and the agony in the Garden of Gethsemane. They expected me to tell them of the spiritual glories of the resurrected life, but I could remember only the shame of the cross of Calvary. Before my departure I had prayed to experience the cross in Israel. Now I can see that God had answered my prayer. I can also say that the cross is not some romantic cosmic concept . . . it is true death.

I returned home a dead man. All my vocational ideas were gone. All my theories of contemplative and active life were gone. I literally could not remember them! All that remained was a love for my simple and humble Lord. All that remained were the visions he had given me. I am to be humble and simple. I am to live a life of poverty so others may be wealthy. I am to live a life of silence in solitary prayer so others may hear the word of God and live in a community of unified love. I am to go forth in apostolic poverty, clad with the habit of the poor, armed with the sword of love, and gifted with a gift of a troubadour for the Lord so that others might receive the gift God gives me in solitude. Above all, I am to love others as he has loved me. I am to forgive as I have been forgiven. I am to be human with others as he has been human with me. I can remember only that he told me to sell all I have, as I have done. I can remember only that I am to clothe myself in the religious habit of a poor man, as I have done. I can remember only that I am to minister the music God gave me as a gift with others, as I have done. However, I can also remember that my ministry was to be carried forth on foot from church to church . . . this has not yet been fully accomplished. Nor has the original community of the vision been fully realized.

It is a conflict with these last two areas that I now face after having returned home. My theories and rationalizations have, in a sense, been erased. I see only an inconsistency between a literal interpretation of God's call for me from these visions and the reality of my actions.

I would like very much for my active ministry in music to leave me available to minister to the needs of the local Franciscan community, not to mention my primary vocation of ministering to the Lord Jesus through contemplative prayer in solitary silence. Originally, I had not envisioned myself with any kind of leadership capacity in this Franciscan community. I thought of myself only as a contemplative hermit who would be involved in the community as a type of catalyst who prompted the real leaders on to holiness and love. This is largely due to my personal feelings of inadequacy and my fears of screwing up other people's lives. I simply don't consider myself a worthy candidate for leadership roles. I have failed in leadership roles in the past due to my young age and my immature conceit, and I simply don't want to fail again. I am still too young, and I am still too egotistical. I need to be led, not to lead. I need to be guided, not to guide. I need to learn, not to teach.

But lately, many people have asked me to make myself more available for active leadership in this Franciscan lay community. In fact, they have scolded me for my hesitance to become involved. Perhaps they are right. Perhaps my fear of failure is only further egotism under the guise of so-called humility.

This leadership capacity within the Franciscan lay community also affects my solitary contemplative vocation. Whereas before I saw the hermitage more or less as a permanent dwelling from which I would come forth but occasionaly, now I must see it as a place for personal retreat and renewal that I would enter into periodically. It would still be the primary residence for my contemplative vocation, but my active vocation might necessitate my being more available to outside communication. This will probably be an ever-present tension that will exist in my overall Franciscan vocation. I must be careful to keep the tension properly balanced so that the line between keeping my vocation strong and snapping it altogether is not crossed.

I must also consider my financial responsibility both to my daughter from my past marriage and to my disabled parents. Since the remarriage of my ex-wife, the financial and moral obligation to my daughter is not as strict as it was, for in practical reality she now has a new father. But my responsibility to my parents is very real, especially considering the present inability of either my brother or sister to aid them in time of need. Scripturally, I must forsake them and honor them by supporting them financially. I must follow God's call for me to poverty, so others may be wealthy, realizing all the while that charity must begin within the Christian family if it is to be truly Christian. Again, with a balance; I must both forsake and honor my family if I would truly please God with real love that is both human and divine.

My extra-local music ministry is the main source for meeting my parent's needs. While I don't ask financial payment to minister, it is usually offered. And while it is not always a great sum, it is sufficient to support most families. Since taking my vow of poverty, I personally need very little; all I therefore make is used to help the needy. Since my father's disabling illness, my parents are the needy. If I give up my extra-local ministry altogether, I would cut off my supply of financial support to my parents. In doing this, I would break one of God's main commandments of love, but in ministering God's love in music for purely financial reasons, I would also break a main commandment of love. So what is the answer?

I believe the answer lies in keeping my entire vocation in a spiritual perspective, rather than in a financial perspective. If I can truly forsake my family, then, and only then, will I be able to honor them. As this relates to my extra-local music ministry, the meaning becomes clear: the extra-local music ministry can validly exist only when both my contemplative and my local active ministries are free to exist. This means it must be cut back considerably in quantity. Then, Lord willing, even its quality will increase both organizationally and spiritually.

As in the beginning of this journal, I still question the validity of my extra-local ministry. I simply minister on the paradox of love in Jesus. There is little to be said about it really. Love must be experienced and then practiced if it is true. Little can be said about it, except by the Word who is living. Only he can speak about it, for only he gives it. And only he gives it correctly, for only he knows the complete interior life of those who are to be loved. I can speak only when he speaks, and when he speaks of true love, I am inclined to give my heart and my actions rather than words. Human words often spring forth from human ideas, while the divine Word of love usually is heard by human actions. In my ministering the simplicity of love, my words are often weak, and my audiences are still conditioned by cultural evangelism to expect strong words of power. I feel my words are powerful. But the listener must be enlightened by the Spirit of Power if he or she is to recognize the power in the weak little words of love. Few understand this Power from on high. We still expect God's kingdom of power in worldly terms, when the New Covenant sets up God's kingdom of power in heavenly terms. Most of us still have our eyes fixed on this world. Most of us do not know the fullness of Jesus, for we do not know the paradoxical power of love.

I guess I have just answered my own question. (Journals are so therapeutic!) It is true that many will not understand me, but I must preach anyway. Let me preach, however, by the action of my worship, rather than by the words of my oratory. Let me show worshipful love by becoming nothing, so that he might be all. Let my sins be confessed, so that he might be found holy. Let my lips be silent, so that the lips of his Spirit might speak. Let my weakness be seen, so that his power will be even more clearly seen.

I must also briefly mention my apostolate in recording. Since the recording of "The Lord's Supper," my new direction in music has a visible manifestation in wax. My ideas concerning worship, art, entertainment, and liturgy have become reality. Of course, I plan to improve on the shortcomings of this work in future works, if the Lord wills. They say "The Lord's Supper" will be quite successful. That would certainly make my extra-local ministry more effective concerning church sponsorship. It would also meet the needs of my parents financially. But only time will tell. It would be nice to continue this new musical direction on record in the future. This would leave me more freedom to become involved in local ministry, while at the same time pruning my extra-local ministry so that it, too, will be more fruitful.

To sum up: the trip to Israel has caused me to reevaluate my entire vocation. The development of potential leadership in the local Franciscan community, not to mention the potential success of my recording apostolate, has also entered into my considerations. I will perhaps now be able more fully to complete God's call for me to work locally, both in lay religious community and in parish churches. The further pruning of my extra-local music ministry will cause both it and my local ministry to be more fruitful. Moving more into local ministry in the Franciscan community, parishes, and album projects is likely, plus continuing my contemplative life in a more organized fashion.

With all of this I am truly amazed. It has all developed so quickly, and seemingly on its own. I have sought only the life of a solitary Franciscan hermit. I honestly thought that was the entire vocation for this part of my life. Then I found that just when I began to fulfill this contemplative call, God dumped all these other possible fulfillments of other calls right into the middle of my peaceful little hermitage. I have no choice but to follow the calls of God if I am in fact professing the love of God. I continue to ask the prayers of Mary, St. Francis, the angels, and all the saints both living and dead so that I might remain humble, simple, and obedient to love. In Jesus' name. Amen.

April 2, 1979—3:00 P.M.—Alverna

The goodness of the Most High is real! He has descended in triumphant humility, and it is this that deemed him worthy to ascend the heights of glory! King of Kings, King of Glory, Lord of Hosts, the Giver of Love, Giver of Life, Prince of Peace, Wonderful Counselor.

Today, I am overjoyed by his reality! By his love. By his humility. By his goodness. By his faithfulness in answering prayer.

I have spent the last few days rapt in the charism of the gospel and the example of St. Francis. Let me seek the warmth of Jesus in coming to love the cold. Let my feet be clad in the protecting sandals of poverty as I feel the life of mother earth caress me. Let me seek the glory of a King by begging alms door to door as a pauper. Let me sing in the finest concert hall by singing in exchange for my food and by sharing my song with all the spring creatures of the wooded hills. The cold will not harm me if I give my life to her. Harm is only in the mind of the harmed. No creature can take from you what you give them freely. I give my blood, my life, my health, my pride, my possessions to all creation. I long only to caress you as you caress me. So come, sister cold and brother hunger. Come, brother shame and sister humility. Come, mother nature and lady poverty. Come, brother Jesus and Father Spirit. Come, all of you. I await the joy of your love and the freedom of your discipline so that I might be fully prepared to meet my brother called sickness and my sister called death.

April 4, 1979—8:30 P.M.—Alverna

Started out as a slow, lazy day of cloudy skies and drizzle-laden woods. I spent most of the day studying the apostolic Fathers and practicing classical guitar. I felt close to Jesus all day and carried his peace in my heart. I also talked to a few people today about Jesus and his church, as has seemed to be the pattern since my return from Israel.

Toward the end of the day, however, I began to feel as if I would never see my daughter again. Somehow I just knew my time in her little life is now over, or at least drawing to a close. I feel the presence of this "religious" father of hers might just complicate her life further. Her mother has chosen another father for her. She must now love and obey him. My presence might create a problem in her personal security that comes from trusting her parents unquestionably. I hope that someday I will again know my little girl. For now, I pray that my presence in body or in spirit will not hurt her further, for I love her more than words can express.

This also led me to consider the First Order again. I love the friars very much and enjoy their company as brothers in community. I long for mature community, and the friars possess a way of life long tried and tested. They are practical and loving. Plus they are not overly pious. They are real . . . most of the time.

But just as I was considering their good points, I came face-to-face with their bad. After they had just come out of a community workshop in psychology, I had to eat with them. The conversation was just a bunch of sophisticated foolishness. They were trying so hard to be real, they appeared to be false. They suddenly reminded me of a group of men who, because they had been deprived of normal development and maturity in the real world, now fill their lives with a so-called intellectual "reality" that is, in truth, unreal. Never having to deal with real sexuality, they now philosophize about "the sexual celibate." Never having to deal with blatant materialism, they now rationalize all luxury under the guise of "poverty of spirit." Never doing business in the real world of roles and games, they now play a game at deciphering the "roles" of those who are attempting to step out of the game. It is all a bunch of religious crap! Some consider themselves wise, but are fools; some spiritually mature, but are emotional children. They have become complex in seeking simplicity and simple-minded in aiding those trapped by true complexity.

109

So back to square one. My idea has faded and is perhaps in its proper place. I still love the friars and submit to them. Their Order is still closest to my heart, and perhaps I, someday, will truly be embraced in their community. But today I must follow God's call in living the Franciscan way toward the simplicity of Jesus. This way includes Francis, but not the friars. I must remain only their "little brother."

I guess what I am trying to say is that I must continue at least to try to live the simplicity of the literal gospel that was so manifest in both the primitive Christian church and the primitive Franciscan Order. The foolishness of the cross alone, and that alone, should be the wisdom of our mystical and practical faith. Now I do not condemn the Franciscans of today's First Order, for the radical call of St. Francis is not practical when literally observed by a large community in modern culture. For them, as with all Christians, poverty in spirit (or the spirit of the gospel) must be applied in varying ways and in varying circumstances. But it is a shame when (and if) the friars inwardly condemn one who is, at least, trying to live the primitive Franciscan life in a literal interpretation of the gospel. This inner resentment and condemnation leads to factions and divisions in the Order.

I do not want to see that happen to an Order I love so much and to which I owe so much. This is why I choose to stay simply a little brother in the Third Order. I do not condemn, and I pray that I am not condemned. I am certainly far from living up to my ideals perfectly, but at least I try. By the grace of Jesus I just might, one day, succeed in living in the charismatic freedom of St. Francis. So in spirit I share a common charism with the friars. In body, I might also share a common work. But it is the soul that is different. They are now mature, rational realists concerning poverty, while I am still the immature, romantic idealist. They realistically accept a less radical application, while I press on for the strict ideal . . . many times both to their and to my disappointment when I can go no further than the rational norm.

I still feel sad. It all has to do with my relationship with the friars. I feel they think me a fool for attempting what I attempt. I feel they think themselves superior simply because they are friars and I am one of the "lesser" brothers of the "impure" stock . . . "secular" not "religious." They would say my sorrow is just psychological paranoia (and perhaps it is), but I do not think so . . . I have lived among them long enough to recognize a spirit "amiss" in the community. It is real. Granted, I have failed to live up fully to my ideals. I am sure I have not heard God's voice in all things he has called me to, but I have tried my best to listen. And where have I not followed the gospel? I own nothing. All I earn is given to the poor. I spend time in solitary prayer. I study the origins of the faith. I labor at a craft and a ministry. I deny myself all luxury, all rest, all fame. Where do I differ from the friars? Only in that their poverty is without risk, owing to the temporal security that comes with their numbers. They are guaranteed all luxury, all security, and even fame by the Order.

I walk this way alone, as Francis first did, taking the real risk of poverty in owning nothing and seeking no security or fame. I differ also in that I have been a man of the world. I have known the good and the bad of worldly fame. I have seen the best and the worst of love, marriage, and the real responsibility of raising a real family. I have been both rich and poor. But I did all these things honestly by 'fessing up to the personal responsibility of living a real life in a real world. I did not profess poverty and then live in wealth, profess humility and live in pride, profess wisdom and live as a fool. I was what I was! I called my life by its true name . . . sin.

So where might I improve? Why am I judged against the early primitive Franciscan ideals by complex, contemporary friars who come no closer to them than I? I have never judged them, neither with my lips nor with my heart . . . even though many do. Why do

I feel this condemnation? But if I love them in Christ, I must try to please them in Christ, regardless of their judgment. If their judgment is real and just, I must improve anyway. Then will their condemnation be unjust, if it still exists. I truly hope this condemnation I feel is just my imagination or a spiritual battle. It hurts me to think that the community I love and respect so much is condemning me behind my back, or even in their innermost thoughts. However, I must be willing to forsake all men if I am truly to love them in heavenly love. I must also consider real vocational improvement, just in case their vocational condemnation is both real and justified. I do this in submission to the friars I love. I pray it is not in pride.

I have been deeply moved by the Franciscan vocation of begging. I have always considered it foolish and unrealistic in its slavish lack of self-sufficiency; so I have never seriously considered it before. However, in the last few days, I have experienced a deep call to the self-sufficient freedom of it . . . the total detachment of it from pride, from comfort, and from money. Can you imagine begging door to door, exchanging a song of praise for some leftover food? It would require wisdom of incredible detachment from the world, for truly the world would attach a foolish label to you if you did it. The detachment from the world required in the religious beggar is precisely the characteristic that would make his or her ministry to the world most effective. This attitude of detachment is possible in other valid ways of expression, but the work of begging appears to be a sure-fire way to test and try whether or not the attitude is true or false.

April 23, 1979—11:45 A.M.—Hermitage

Much has been happening. Both my contemplative life and my active life have been prosperous. Prayer life is good. Manual labor is good. Albums are good. Concerts are good. And the lay community of secular Franciscans is good.

Father Martin counseled me to try mendicant begging but to remain in my concert ministry. At the same time, my concert ministry is being pruned back to my original plan of only one week per month for sponsors interested in working with the Catholic Church and the "Charity" program. It looks like the time problem is being worked out both externally and interiorly. My attitude has become more charitable concerning my apostolate. It also appears that the situation with the friars is getting better. This is because God has been dealing with my attitude, I suppose, and he has probably dealt with their attitudes as well.

God is dealing with the lay Franciscans in general as well as with me alone concerning mendicant living. Many in this community are being called to a mendicant apostolate. For married people and people with jobs, this means a door-to-door apostolate of visitation and concern within local parishes. Coupled with attending Mass regularly and other spiritual, educational, and social parish work, this could be quite effective. I myself would like to be involved in this aspect of the evangelization program proposed by the church.

Jesus is also calling some people to live the early Franciscan life of poverty and prayer in a more radical sense. Many people are coming to me, wanting to embark on the mendicant life of solitary prayer and preaching, supported on a day-to-day basis of picking up odd jobs and begging in return for food and a place to sleep. I am tempted to ask permission to open up my hermitage to other little brothers interested in this life. Little sisters could sleep in the back room of the prayer chapel we are now planning to build. I could ask the friars if they might work in the building of this chapel and in the planting and keeping of herb, flower, and vegetable gardens here at Alverna in exchange for leftover food. They would all be expected to work door-to-door from time to time in both begging and home visitation.

This literal mendicant life is strange. It is not the alternative life for all Christians. It is only a catalyst for others. It is only the leaven of the dough. But it is this life, like the life of the early apostles and friars, that aids in the active process of creating the new bread that serves as an alternative life-style for all Christians.

The people called to this life are usually unhappy as long as they do not radically follow the call. They are often chanelled into Orders or fellowships that attempt to rationalize the outer call of mendicancy, while retaining the inner flavor of it. While this channeling is good for the majority, it is not good to the few who have been truly chosen for this unusual charism. As long as they do not radically respond, they remain in a state of inner unrest and often degenerate into totally unstable people. This is because their superiors have not allowed for this charism because of the risk involved in being called "unusual."

The primitive mendicant charism has almost disappeared from religious life in America. We must allow the few called to this life to embark upon their vocation with the full support of the church, so that the majority of Christians may prosper from their radical example. Then both the leaven and the dough will work together so that the Body of Christ may rise heavenward and feed those of this earth with heavenly Bread.

Perhaps it is the forming of this radically mendicant community that would solve both my problem and theirs. Working together, much could be accomplished in a short period of time. The time problem would be solved for my vocational calls, plus their need for support in this life could be met. I will ask the friars about this idea to find the mind of God.

April 25, 1979—11:15 A.M.— *Indianapolis Airport*

I have had some good days in the hermitage. It was good for me just to listen to the wind and the water for a few days. I got to know some of my animal neighbors, as well as brother and sister squirrel who are quite curious about my presence in the woods.

114

They spend their afternoons in the tree right outside my door, watching me as I work. The chipmunk, too, is getting to know me from his hiding place in my woodpile—upon which I lean as I soak in both the sun and the rain. There is also a family of ducks who frequent the creek, and they also are not afraid of me. It was good to see brother snake on the rocks a few days ago. He will be harmless as always, I am sure. My wood-cutting is getting on well, and large piles are slowly accumulating where once there were only small piles scattered in the woods. This time in the hermitage helped balance my increased activity both in local and in extralocal ministry. Times of solitude, silence, and listening truly enrich and stabilize our times of activity among people in charity and proclamation. My activity has also been good lately, but it has been truly active. I have been going over contracts and future recording plans, not to mention the offers coming in for me to minister in music. There is a pattern developing that I believe is truly God working in the plan of this active ministry.

First, regarding contracts, I think God is pleased with people making definite and clear covenants with one another when prompted by mutual love and trust. But to make far-reaching plans for the future and to let the civil authorities be the judge and executioner in case of default is not in keeping with the words of Jesus concerning Christian planning and Christian authority in case of dispute. I feel comfortable with an album-by-album agreement that is to be judged by the church authority in case of default by either party. This leaves freedom for the Holy Spirit to move in various ways at various times with various people, and it allows the Holy Spirit to judge God's people through the Church of Jesus and the people he himself has placed in authority.

There are two major developments concerning my extra-local ministry. First, in dealing with autonomous promoters and fellowships, I am finding the crowds and ministry to be good, but the financial aspect to be bad. Offerings are good, but expenses are far too high, owing to lack of local unity and day-to-day effectiveness by these autonomous promoters and fellowships. They must promote by media rather than by word of mouth, and the simple day-to-day witness of effective and solid Christian love in the Church community. So I am finding that they do not even pay my expenses when I minister for them. I believe this is a sign that I am to stop playing for these people, especially when God has told me to play only for credible sponsors who are interested in unity and a return to early church catholicity. Which leads me to my second point: with the success of "The Lord's Supper" album, many such Catholic sponsors are calling to ask me to come to their area and minister. I believe I will shortly be able to play almost exclusively for inter-denominational renewal activities coming forth from the structure of the Catholic Church. The charismatic renewal and the Franciscan Order co-sponsoring the "Charity" program with other Catholic-minded fellowships seems to be a very real alternative to my past situation. With all of this, I must simply recognize that Jesus doesn't ask you to do something unless he plans on helping you to do it. He appears to be making this change for me, since I was too cowardly to do it myself. I thank him for his grace, his forgiveness, and his love.

The success of "The Lord's Supper" is also quite awesome. It appears that it is a "hit" by most standards. This awes me beyond words. What this means is simply that I could stand to make a lot of money from royalties. Relative to my vow of poverty, this leaves interesting possibilities for putting the money to good use. It also means that, relative to helping my parents and my daughter, I might not have to play extra-locally too much longer. This means I can afford to cut back to unity-oriented ministries (assuming the autonomous sponsors might take a turn for the better owing to the success of the album).

April 27, 1979—Alverna

The concert ministry since Easter has failed financially while still prospering in proclaiming the gospel spiritually.

Last night was another such failure, except last night I was accused of not preaching the gospel as well. I simply read the words of Jesus directly from the Gospel according to Luke, commenting very briefly at the end of a long reading. I spoke of the loving commitment that prompts us to die for one another so another might live. I spoke of the paradox of the cross. I spoke the message of the gospel of Jesus as understood by men and women of Jesus through the ages. I didn't speak in accordance with some self-proclaimed prophet's interpretation of the "Gospel According to American Prosperity." Consequently, this poor troubadour raised some of those American Christian's eyebrows in the simple preaching of the gospel. In other words, I didn't say "give to get in return," but rather give out of a love that expects nothing in return and you will receive reward in your giving. In fact, I was accused of negating the Christian ministry in this town. These brothers are sincere, and much of their message is needed to balance other lopsided messages heard today. But when their message is applied dogmatically to the point of negating the very words of Jesus, it becomes nothing short of error and false prophecy. I pray God will balance all teachings in the wisdom of love.

This experience simply reinforced God's call to me, in light of the dilemma of supporting these private interpretations and self-proclaimed prophets, by coming to a town under their sponsorship. I must now leave this aspect of the music ministry once and for all. I intend to cancel all such dates in the future, and accept only requests by more Catholic-oriented sponsors, sympathetic to the contemporary charismatic renewal and the message of early church spirituality of past tradition. Only then will I contribute to Spirit-filled and orthodox ministries. Only then will I be obedient.

April 28, 1979—10:30 P.M.—Alverna

An eventful day! In fact, an eventful two days! It started by my father exploding over a financial question in my concert ministry and telling me I should quit altogether. He did this out of love for me. Then my mother voiced her concerns about my ideals and ended by telling me that she felt my mendicant and contemplative life is self-centered and egotistical. She did this out of love for me and in an attempt to understand my thinking. Then I showed a real lack of judgment in dealing with my pregnant sister when she refused to respond to loving exhortations to obey the doctor's orders. I finally had to resort to being angry in trying to get her back in bed, but this totally backfired by sending her to bed in hysterics.

All of this culminated by making me totally aware of my inability to handle responsibility. I have failed as a husband. I have failed as a son and brother. I am now scared to death of failing in my religious calling as both active and contemplative. There is this ugly strain of selfishness and rational self-confidence that has plagued my Christian life for nearly nine years. It kills all it touches, unless covered by God's grace. I must be sure to follow God's call, lest I kill those I love as well.

Some people have told me that I am called of God to become a musical voice, both to and from the Catholic Church. This frightens me to the depths of my soul. I cannot deny God's anointing of the album ministry, but the place of recognition I receive from this anointing seems unwarranted. I see my sin of pride and selfishness. I see my failure as a Christian and as a human being. I see my foolishness and become frightened of such recognition, both for my sake and the sake of my ministry in the church. I see all this and realize that I must get my life together soon in God's grace, or else God's grace will finally totally withdraw from my life and my ministry, leaving me in the torment of despair and total failure.

This evening I instituted a clear program concerning my contemplative life and my active ministry. After bearing the punishment of my past leniencies in booking, I will undertake a clearly defined but limited apostolate. The contemplative aspect of my life will again become my priority, as is fitting a true mendicant. Gardening, wood-chopping, and begging will provide my food and shelter. I will leave time for both study and prayer every day.

I will do penance for my sins so that I might never forget my frailty and my need for God's grace. Only then will I undertake an active apostolate in music, and then only from a proper structure with both proper purpose and proper ethics. It is only by following this discipline of penance and prayer that I might safely receive any authority God might choose to give me. God gave me the gift, and he told me how I was to share it. If I share it improperly, he will surely make the gift ineffective, if not take it from me completely. I pray for God's grace so I might follow my Jesus both to the cross of his death and to the resurrection of his eternal life.

April 29, 1979—9:00 A.M.*—Alverna*

It feels good to rest in Godly order.

April 30, 1979—5:35 P.M.*—* *Indianapolis Airport*

On my way to L.A. to work on sheet-music finalizing and contract agreements. It has been a good day.

A new peace has come to me for the first time since my return from Israel. Jesus has shown me why I was not at peace and what I must do to enter into his peace again. It all simply has to do with moderate discipline.

Through circumstances and my own negligence, this spring has been very busy and very unorganized. Too many days of hectic activity, with too few days of peaceful prayer. There have been days off, but the responsibility of preparing for active days destroyed much of my contemplation. Contracts, telephones, unexpected visitors, and the mental demands of trying to organize unorga-

119

nized projects have made the simple work of still and quiet worship of God very difficult.

So the return to a moderate discipline, or at least pinpointing the problem, has brought a new inner peace and freedom. Limiting the quality and quantity of my apostolate in the music ministry is the answer to the problem. Moderately following all my vocational calls will fulfill them. But trying to follow any one of them exclusively destroys them all through fanaticism.

There is a big difference between the radical and the fanatic. The radical Christian returns to the original simplicity of love that, in turn, brings about holy poverty and prayerful penance. The fanatic simply returns to outer poverty and exterior penance without being properly motivated by love. The radical Christian meets the extreme challenge of a life of faith and commitment with an inner peace that permeates his entire life and all those he touches. The fanatic meets the extreme challenge with a cold and harsh zealousness that in the end throws both himself and those he meets into confusion and inner frustration.

I think I have recently been on the brink of fanaticism. All radicals can easily become fanatics without experiencing the grace of Jesus' love. I have become too caught up in the externals of my vocation, and have discovered that my interior peace has been jeopardized. I have discovered that I am becoming increasingly cold-hearted regarding both God and men. In emphasizing the outer loving actions, I have nearly forgotten the inner loving attitude. I have nearly become a "whitened sepulchre" like the pharisees of Jesus' time, always willing to give, but never able to love. Only the grace of Jesus' Spirit in our life can enable us to love as God originally intended us to love. I must daily make an effort to know him in his love; then the true ascetic vocation of the contemplative mendicant will follow in its own due time.

May, 1979—8:40 P.M.—
Kansas City Airport

I am still on my L.A. trip, only two hours from home. I have visited Sparrow Records, Keith Green, and Jerry Bryant's community, and John Clauder of the S.C.R.C. (Southern California Renewal Communities). The album is doing quite well, with 25,000 sold in three and one-half weeks. The prospects for videotaping and further classically oriented works are truly exciting. I also really enjoyed Keith's community. I sense a maturing in Keith that tempered the imperfection of his new zeal. S.C.R.C. is planning a beautiful convention at the Anaheim Convention Center for the charismatic renewal in southern California. I felt an incredible kinship with their vision concerning humble submission to the church and the integration of the contemplative tradition into the renewal of today. But my visit with them stirred up the old leadings to a strict mendicant living that fluctuates between solitude and the wanderings of a mendicant pilgrim. I sensed their longing for a contemporary leader in this area. Somehow, I feel God has chosen me for this.

My music will not reach the church until I totally withdraw from both music and direct ministry to the church. Record . . . yes. Work occasionally in local parishes . . . yes. But the large ministries seem far beyond me. I will not be worthy of legitimately contributing to those kinds of ministries until I have spent years in local community and in strict times of solitude. I have much to learn about prayer, about theology, and about music. I will not stand legitimately as a liturgist and a teacher until I have had more experience. God has anointed the album apostolate. God has anointed the lay community and my contemplative vocations in solitude. But I still feel a blocking to the apostolate of large gatherings. I feel totally unworthy. No . . . premature. I feel like a bride who is marrying too soon, or sleeping in bed with a temporary lover. I just want to

121

make sure I am saving my treasure for my Bridegroom. I want fully to follow the Lord Jesus in his footsteps. I must beware of straying from the path of his will.

May 14, 1979—Denver

A good week of ministry. Prisons, churches, and a few major concerts. I have also met a whole bunch of people with lovely hearts and sweet dispositions. Some good people in the Catholic renewal and some equally good people open to working with Catholics. Jesus is moving in his entire Body to bring us back to unity.

Interiorly I still feel the call to order and solitude. I am sure that only by withdrawing into solitude will I be able truly to minister to the active Body. It is a great mystery, but I know it is true. My albums have been anointed by the Spirit and the Spirit is fully capable of anointing many people, both to listen and to come into worship through the albums. Many people I spiritually respect have confirmed this in the Lord. I feel good about it!

May 26, 1979—12:00 Noon—Alverna

Cold days. It is beautiful to behold the sun and the clear sky, but it is a bit chilly to be out and around. I have been up the hill in the room with my reference books, studying philosophy, theology, and music. It feels good to study again. It makes me feel a bit more "grounded" after months away from a serious discipline of study. It will also prepare me for a Bible study I am supposed to lead for some friends in the future. I feel very "monastic" today, not like a hermit or a Franciscan. I am wearing a new summer habit. Perhaps its newness and neatness are influencing my attitude. Oh well, it too will be old and worn soon, just like the good ol' habit of my first vocational winter.

May 29, 1979—6:30 A.M.*—Alverna*

God has given me a word about the dispersion, or the incomplete unity of his spiritual Israel, the church. In the dispersion of physical Israel, many Jews lived lives of health and prosperity, even enjoying religious freedom in their sojourn in a pagan land. From all objective perspectives, they often lived a more blessed life during the dispersion than during the times when they were gathered in a unity within the physical boundaries of the homeland God had given them. But God desired that they be a nation, so God called them out of dispersion after the appointed time to return to the original homeland of Israel. But owing to the comfort of their life in dispersion, many did not respond. Only about ten percent of the Jews returned to Israel to try and rebuild the holy city Jerusalem and the holy temple of sacrifice and worship on Mount Moriah.

And why should they return? Must a spiritual God be worshiped in a physical homeland? After all, Israel was but a wasteland destined to be a military outpost of every great nation coming and going between Europe and Africa for many years gone by and for many years to come. It was a cursed land by all objective observations. They were better off, both physically and spiritually, just where they were . . . or so they thought. So, few returned at first out of the dispersion of Israel. Yet God desired that they return to the original homeland and establish the physical burdens of Israel once more.

The same holds true for the church of Jesus, the people of the New Covenant, the spiritual Israel. In the Great Schism and the Reformation, God judged the stiff-necked clergy of the church by sending her laity into dispersion. Now, after many generations, God is calling his New Covenant people back to the original homeland of early church catholicity, so they may be a nation again—clearly visible within the boundaries of a unified doctrine and a unified hierarchical government. Then will God's people truly enter into a unified worship of him. But, just as with the physical Israel, the dispersed spiritual Israel has grown comfortable in her dispersion. She enjoys great health and prosperity as generation after generation are free to worship God as they see fit. Great churches have arisen that are fat with spiritual health and prosperity. Love abounds, as Jesus said it would, but unity is seldom seen, for each city of dispersion "sees fit" differently. Therefore, the witness of love is defamed.

But as the children of dispersion look back to the boundaries of their motherly homeland, the Catholic Church, they see only a wasteland that has often been the scene of military battle. Why should they return? Is not Jesus a spiritual God for all nations? After all, the dispersion is not that bad, is it? But God is calling the dispersed people home, so they might worship Jesus as a unified nation with clear boundaries of doctrine and clear leadership in government. He calls us now to rebuild a unified temple of love and worship of Jesus our Lord and Savior. A few have returned, but many more must follow if the wasteland is to be cultivated, watered, weeded, and come to bear much fruit again.

June 3, 1979—10:30 A.M.—Alverna

Some good developments here at Alverna. We are beginning to work on a prayer chapel for the lay Franciscans. It is the old toolshed that was originally a chapel. We are simply restoring it to its original purpose. We will also use its original name, "Portiuncula," or "The Little Portion." This ties in well with the idea for the Third Order house of prayer. We are the "little portion" and the "little brothers and sisters" here at Alverna. We must serve and obey, not be served and obeyed. Our ministry is small, personal ministry to just a few at a time who seek direction concerning contemplative prayer, apostolic poverty of spirit, and the overall outworking of Jesus' love in their life. We also are making ourselves

124

available as lay people to lead basic studies in scripture on practical Christian living. Not studies requiring the theology of a priest, but simply the basics of dedicated lay people helping other lay people out of love. We also have a new resident, thus realizing the "outer care" idea of temporary residents, coming here to experience the blessings and hardships of a more contemplative lay community.

Personally, I feel good, but I am getting a bit bogged down in study. I need, now, to balance this objective study with contemplative times of prayer. Not that I do not set aside many hours during the day for prayer. I just need to divorce myself from study during times of prayer. Oh, well, the pendulum swings "as a pendulum do."

June 8, 1979—10:30 A.M.*—Alverna*

The pendulum began to swing too far back the other way, but God saved me from swinging out too far. Study was beginning to consume me. I was beginning to think of myself as a teacher rather than a man of prayer. I felt the weight of the entire local community's need for teaching on my back. It was awful! Then Jesus reminded me of my real vocation and of his promise of working through the Body. So I can return to prayer as my main vocation, thus keeping study in its proper place. Yes, I must die even to study before I can aptly teach. I must seek only to pray if I am to teach in his Spirit.

June 10, 1979—8:15 A.M.*—Alverna*

Just had a meeting with Catholics interested in extended households yesterday. It became clearer in that meeting that few

Catholics know what they are, or why they are what they are. As in the analogy of the regathering of spiritual Israel, the church: some of God's people were not dispersed. A few stayed in Israel. But those who stayed were worse off than many of those who enjoyed comfort in dispersion. Today, many born Catholics are like those who were not dispersed, staying behind in a battle-torn, oppressed Israel. The only reason they stay within the borders of the nation is that they were born within those borders. Yet, in the backs of their minds, when they hear of the success of some of the dispersed brethren, they wish that they too had been carried off to some wealthy nation. They may be within the borders, but many of them have yet to hear God's voice calling a people to return to the homeland and establish a nation.

So in truth they are often less a part of the nation seeking full unity than those who are, at least, looking for the real borders from a distant place of dispersion. God desires his Body to be unified both spiritually and physically, yet he calls us heart-to-heart, whether we be already within the physical borders of the homeland or dispersed in some faraway land. God seeks our heart first, and then the borders of the homeland will serve their true purpose. Many within the borders are further from a heartfelt regathering than those who are yet many physical miles distant from the borders of physical Israel, the Catholic Church.

July 1, 1979—Alverna

Have worked out more vocational problems concerning "Little Portion" at Alverna. Through the direction of the friars, we have established that we are a "house of prayer," not a halfway house. Our ministry is loving prayer, not social action. We may take in temporary guests for up to ten days at a time, but only those who need a time of prayer to reexamine their lives, not those who need extended psychological help. We should continue to love all who come to us, but we must realize our limitations in ministering to all, so that we can truly help a few. Otherwise we would be wasting everyone's time.

July 26, 1979—Alverna

Back from a charismatic convention in southern California. Got a chance to meet a lot of people I have respected for quite some time. This includes some Camaldolese postulants from Big Sur. In talking to them, I discovered they are much more flexible than I thought. A limited apostolate under guidance is permitted when it is an obvious work of the Holy Spirit. Of course, their more strict house in Ohio disagrees with this, and in light of monastic history, I am not so sure it is good for their Order, even though it is in line with my own personal vocation. Either way, I did not feel God calling me to their Order at this time. I loved the spirit of the brothers, and I would love to spend some time with them when I am in California, but it is not a permanent vocation for me. After all, they wear a white habit . . . the one Jesus gave me is brown. There is both an exterior and an interior difference in our vocational clothing.

Regarding my input into the convention, I was quite pleased at the reception I received. I felt I had something good to share with the renewal, and I was happy that they received me with love and joy. The contemplative spirit of peace and love flowed through my music and was willingly received by most who listened. It is good to see the renewal receptive to contemplative spirituality.

It is just this point that prompts me to guard my contemplative vocation further against too much active ministry. It is the contemplative aspect of my music that causes my activity to be successful; yet too much activity will surely destroy the contemplative life that gives life to my music. I must guard my private time with Jesus that takes me to the heights of the contemplative kingdom, so

127

I might more successfully shout his message of love from the house-tops—into the streets of the world.

I must also express my fear, or awe, of God's wonder. Being placed in such a place of public recognition does scare me. I feel like a mere babe who has been asked to run with the assuredness of a mature man.

July 27, 1979—Alverna

Had a good talk with Father Martin about a contemplative house of prayer at Alverna. He said that after August/September, it could be a viable possibility. He will speak to Cheri and me in detail next week sometime.

August 2—Feast of the Portiuncula—Alverna

A beautiful day of work and prayer. The day started with a small dedication Mass in the new prayer chapel in honor of St. Mary of the Portiuncula. This little chapel is truly a little portion of quiet simplicity and poverty where great visions rich in God's love can begin. With Mary, it has a hidden ministry that not many will consciously know about, yet from the womb of this hidden, quiet chapel of contemplative prayer great works of Jesus' salvation may be openly born into the world. This is what the chapel and the house of prayer are dedicated to.

Spent the first part of my day cleaning the hermitage. Next I worked on scrubbing the floor of the prayer chapel. It was a good time of prayer, as I worked on my knees so the honor of this day might be seen in a small thing like a clean floor.

I then spent several hours by the creek in prayer. Jesus confirmed in my spirit the steps of my vocation. The first step involves contemplative prayer, study, and work, balancing life in community with life in the hermitage. My music apostolate will remain an important part of this stage. The second step involves increasing time in the hermitage to an almost constant vocation; yet music will still remain. The last step involves a pure mendicant life of wandering from church to church as a poor troubadour for the Lord. The last step is maturely entered into only after many years of preparing in the first two steps of my vocation.

September 2, 1979—8:00 P.M.—Alverna

Have learned a little more about my tendency to domestic family, the love sacrifice of celibacy, and the paradox of my love affair with Jesus, my Lover.

I see my daughter and my heart yearns to be a normal father for her. She loves me deeply, and so I too love her deeply; but because of Nancy's remarriage the reality of my being a normal, day-to-day father is impossible. I see my daughter's confusion and hear her little questions that I cannot answer, and I am moved to great sorrow. Her presence stirs a great love and a great pain within us both, so that I am scarcely able to be around her and still keep my composure. I am truly sorry that this little girl must suffer from the mistakes of my youth; yet no matter how sorry I am, it seems that both she and I must suffer this separation that neither of us really wants. This is my life-long penance, I suppose, for whenever I see this little girl I am unable to hold back the tears that well up within the sorrow of my repentant soul.

I feel this same sorrow when I see a holy woman of God who is romantically drawn to me in a mutual attraction that is both natural and spiritual. A woman beautiful in body, soul, and spirit who seeks to fill her inner loneliness with the love of a man of God who suffers the same loneliness. This is not just genital attraction. It is a simple desire for a companion to help fill up empty days and nights.

A lover to share laughter and tears. A lover to share both conversation and silence. A lover to share the inner quiet of the heart. I must admit my desire for a simple domestic woman of God with whom to share my life in God. Yet through the objective law of God's church and the existential call of God on my life, I know that this earthly reward is now impossible for me. I cannot go back to the love of my wife, nor can I go on to the love of another woman. This too is a life-long penance for the mistakes of my youth.

Yet this is the paradox of my love affair with Jesus. It is in my loneliness for him that I find companionship with him, who was ever alone on the cross for me. It is in the passion of this dark night that Jesus and I embrace until the coming of the dawn of morning. The tears of loneliness mingle with the blood of his dying as the water of my humanity is mixed with his divine wine in sacrifice for all the world. I join with him in the agony of the garden as he besought the Father to take this cup of lonely death from him. Yet I also join with him as he submits to the will of the Father. I join with him in the silence before an earthly prince who would gladly have given him earthly reward if he would but ask for the kingdom of the world. Yet I also join with him in the proclamation of the good news, of heavenly love for others among all the nations of this world. So Jesus and I consummate our marriage in the passion of the cross that cries out in loneliness and anguish to the Father of mercy, so that we might both be the ever-present parents of the children of God's mercy. This is the passion of my marriage bed. This is the paradox of my love with Jesus.

September 16, 1979—10:00 A.M.—Alverna

I have been doing some thinking about the house of prayer vocation at Alverna. Many of the friars have commented on the proposed rule of life I wrote for the secular Franciscans at this house of prayer. They usually think the rule is highly spiritual and highly workable, but they object to the "Benedictine" quality of its specific treatment of various questions about community. They think it should be more "Franciscan" by remaining silent concerning these questions, and letting the individual more or less do as he or she pleases. I do not agree with the objection. First, the rule is Franciscan in its flexibility. It deals with the specific questions about community and the contemplative life, but it never does so in a strict way. The whole point of dealing flexibly with these specifics is to insure the flexibility of a Spirit-led individual life within the context of Spirit-led community. The specific nature of the rule is not confining. It is an insurance to preserve freedom in a way that is not nebulous. It is "Benedictine" in its specific treatment, but it is ever "Franciscan" in its insured flexibility.

Secondly, it is truly Franciscan in that it combines the call of the friar and the Poor Clare into one working community of little brothers and sisters. It is based on the stable contemplative life of prayer of the Poor Clare. The community remains primarily contemplative and peacefully ordered, so times of prayer and study will be insured. However, the mendicant call of the friar is also included. As all experience the riches of contemplative prayer in community, various apostolates may be undertaken, as long as the primary contemplative call is not disrupted. This concept of mixed vocations in a community of men and women helps to bring the miracle of the Body of Christ into a fuller manifestation in individual communities, thus giving greater balance and stability to each community.

However, there must be one common call to a life of contemplative prayer among all members of the community, so the strain of unworkable diversity in apostolates will not destroy the workable, common unity of the house of prayer. Likewise, the diversity is good in that it balances the individual human needs and personalities of both men and women in community. But the danger of sexual immorality must be constantly remembered, so the holy call to celibacy will be preserved as we offer ourselves wholly to the love of Jesus, our Divine Lover.

The rule is also very Franciscan in that it is both idealistic and workable. In a time when contemplative vocations are on the decrease in established Orders, in a time when established Orders are having to close down houses and seminaries, the lay people called to a life of humble work and contemplative prayer can join with religious to fulfill a vision much larger than one branch of one Order. By combining efforts, these dying houses could be lovingly healed as part of the Body of Christ and brought to full new life as dynamic spiritual centers. In these centers, the beautiful religious traditions of the past could be preserved within the powerful contemporary move of the Holy Spirit of Jesus that is currently sweeping through both the religious and the laity of this world. As a Franciscan, I see this applying to many such Franciscan places. However, I also see it as applicable within many established Orders with similar problems. I also see this inter-Order openness as a necessary part of Franciscan spirituality.

How I long to just graze in the plenteous pastures of the Shepherd's field in loving unity with the sheep of the fold. Yet it seems I am constantly finding myself in the position of shepherding the flock so all the sheep might be completely gathered into one field and remain forever one in the Good Shepherd's field. I feel unworthy and unable to complete this hard task. I am no shepherd. I am least among the dumbest of sheep. I have no official schooling, no official position, yet here I am speaking to others about the objective and subjective realities of the Sheepfold. I pray God will not find me presumptuous or proud. I pray it is truly his call I have heard in doing this. Lord have mercy on me if I am wrong!

But it seems God is opening all these doors. I have prayed to minister in the church, so God has brought me into the church and then brought the leaders of the church almost to my door. Here at Alverna, I have met and ministered to the clergy of this diocese. I have sung and spoken for the international leaders of the secular Franciscan Order and the friars from distant places. I pray God keep me humble in this premature exaltation.

This international meeting of the secular Franciscan Order was truly encouraging. God is renewing the original call of Jesus and the fervor of the Spirit-led gospel life in this community! I met many wonderful brothers and sisters in Jesus at the meeting. All are so serious about following the leading of the Spirit. All are so serious about living the gospel in community. All are so serious about Jesus! What a cause for rejoicing! I believe renewal is underway!

In the midst of all this, my ministry is going along just the way Jesus promised. It is prospering as I make a conscious effort to make it lowly. God has opened the door to much work in parishes, small groups, home visitation, and visitation of the sick; and along with these lowly ministries, God has caused the large ministries to prosper as well. The album ministry is likewise doing fine. But through all this, God constantly tests and tries my vow of poverty. Praise him for the gift of gospel poverty, so others might know the wealth of the kingdom! I will pass the test by the help of this grace!

Through all this, my prayer life has continued without harm. I have made conscious efforts to take time in each day to just "be" with Jesus. I have been able substantially to persevere in a discipline of prayer, study, and work; so my inner peace prevails even in times of outer chaos. This is good.

December 11, 1979—11:00 P.M.—Alverna

Can't sleep, so I decided to bring the journal up to date. I am working on two new musical projects and planning a trip to Europe. I am leaving for L.A. tomorrow morning to finish a prayer album and to work on overdub and orchestration for a new "Talbot Brothers Album."

As far as my personal vocation and the community are concerned, I see an integration between various past Catholic traditions. I see an integration between religious and secular. I see an integration between monastic and mendicant. I see this integrated community of my vocation as being both male and female (of course, the sleeping quarters of the celibate communities would be separated), active and contemplative, married and celibate. I hope to tap the good of not just one tradition, but of all past community traditions in the church of Jesus. Then will I come closer to being in line with the full work of the Holy Spirit. Then will I, hopefully, please my Father.

Perhaps this Arkansas land I bought so many years ago will someday help fulfill the call Jesus has given me. After working with the Indianapolis Secular Franciscan Order, I thought perhaps the rural and contemplative communities could be realized there. From Indianapolis I could perhaps go out to establish yet more such communities.

I must also include here my growing desire to become a permanent deacon. I do not feel worthy or called to the priesthood, but I sense the desire of full submission to the church in my preaching and ministering. The Diaconate would directly submit me to the Church and would, I feel, strengthen my ministry through the sacramental graces of Jesus and his church. To do this I would have to study for at least two years.

Perhaps between now and the time of the move to Arkansas, I could pursue this course toward the diaconate—while also building up the charismatic Secular Francisican Order community. I might also want to visit some existing monastic communities and stay with them for a while as a "student."

There is a sense of expectancy here at Alverna. Much change in the air. I know we need the approval of the friars before we can accept any new members to the house of prayer, and I feel we will not grow much in the vocation without the support of a few more brothers and sisters living this life with us. We may or may not receive the approval. Alverna has been a good "womb" for my vocational birth, but depending on the decision of the friars, we might need to move on soon.

February 5, 1980—4:00 P.M.—Alverna

Many developments. My father has died, and God has called me back from Europe. I knew I shouldn't go, but I went anyway. I feel my absence at my father's passing is a chastisement for my disobedience to what I know is God's voice within. I am also down with the flu. I feel this, too, is a chastisement from God. Jesus wanted me to spend time at home in solitude, but I went to L.A. to mix a new album instead. All of this is teaching me to listen to God's still, small voice within all the more. I am grateful for this lesson of love. I am a sinner. Lord have mercy.

It appears that the possibility of a "house of prayer" at Alverna is becoming real. Even with growing support for such a community, however, God's voice within calls me to total poverty and abandonment. I am not to seek or "possess" any idea of community. I am not to "build" anything. I am to give all to Jesus. I am to tear down my sin through penance, so Jesus alone might rebuild my life. To live a solitary life of poverty and prayer is all I can seek. I am unworthy to teach others or to share with others. I am worthy only to be taught. God wants me to be his alone, so he alone might teach me. Then, perhaps, I might someday be worthy of sharing in his plans for community. I seek only to die abandoned and alone for the sake of the world, even as our Lord died abandoned and alone for the sake of my soul. For this alone was I created, and in this alone will I be fulfilled. Oh Lord, let me know the grace of this dying!

Epilogue
by Sister Cheri White

Nearly five years have passed since the close of this journal, and nearly seven since I joined John Michael at Alverna in the late summer of 1978. I came across him on the tree-shaded bank of Williams Creek, working quietly to remove old mortar from a pile of used bricks he had begged from the friars to use in building his hermitage. Even then, the air was charged with vision, breaking distant from its depths toward the shore of impending fulfillment in space and time.

In the course of that beginning, the old bricks and some new concrete blocks became John Michael's own hermitage. The "possibility" of a house of prayer at Alverna, mentioned at the close of John's journal, became the Little Portion House of Prayer, that very year in fact, as vision began to take on form. But the Lord works through his imperfect servants, and you can be sure there were many who came and went in those early days who were hard put to know whether we were in the midst of birth pangs or death throes as we struggled to find our balance in the will of God! Yet the Lord was merciful, and at the end of our "House of Prayer" phase, there were six of us living a life of prayer, study, and service in the old carriage house we rented from the friars, who say even now that there are people having treasured experiences alone with God in the crooked-walled hermitage built by a musician's hands.

In 1982, five of us left the protective womb of Alverna during a frosty November, in response to a call for an even greater commit-

136

ment to prayer and solitude. The men and women each rented a house in Eureka Springs, Arkansas, where our metamorphosis continued through the seasons until our hermitages on "the Arkansas land" were completed in late 1983, and we settled in our permanent home as the Little Portion Franciscan Hermitage.

What cannot be told here are the five years' worth of stories that unfolded between those first promptings of God, revealed in this journal, and the appearance of our twelve hermit cells on an Ozark hillside. But be sure that real lives were tested and proven through the entire gamut of circumstances that make up the course of any true spiritual journey. Anger, accusations, frustrations, fears, jealousies, mistrust, unreasonable expectations, and plenty of tears were (and continue to be) transformed through the cross into sacrifice, encouragement, patience, tolerance, trust, assuredness, and joy. We have commited ourselves to letting it happen—to opening our hearts and minds to the often painful and always joyful process of being conformed to the image of Christ.

John Michael's prophetic role, like his music, moves always with the characteristics of an ocean wave: just when you think you know where it is, it has moved back into the sea to roll in somewhere else, but it's still the same ocean. If anything, we have learned as a community to live with this ebb and flow as a normal condition. Projects, resources, anointings, gifts, ministries, and capacities—not to mention people—come and go, changing the shoreline of our communal life as the Lord gives and takes away. And so, John Michael —and the community—continues to struggle with the paradox of his public ministry, which both supports and threatens to destroy our dream all at the same time. Also continuing are his deliberations —and ours—concerning our place in the Franciscan family.

What it all means is that we continue to live with the creative tension that a life-style of quiet and solitude with a ministry in the arts sets up for us, believing that God has called us to it for a purpose. Those resilient people whom God has placed around John Michael have not lived life lightly. Most are refugees from the status quo who have been broken in many ways, whose worldviews demanded that life add up, and who discovered in the end, like John, that it does so only in Jesus Christ. The vision that came through John Michael and extended to the community will extend out to many, apart from him or us, if it is truly from the one true God who continues to search the earth for those who will hear his voice in these times. And the times are ripe for those who will say, and have said, with John Michael: "For this alone was I created, and in this alone will I be fulfilled."

Yet, it is true that we see through a glass darkly, even while striving to walk in the light of the Spirit. Even as the tidal wave of Christ's desire courses through the current of salvation history to break upon our little shore in time, we are often caught standing in the sand when the first wave hits, and are reminded to scramble back onto the Rock where our responses to his soundings will not and cannot be swept away.

Just as Francis ran to gather stones and began to repair a fallen-down structure when the Lord said to him, "Rebuild my Church!" so John Michael, in great symbolic parallel, ran to gather materials to implement the Lord's command to his own obedient heart by building that first small hermit's hut at Alverna. What remained to Francis and remains to John Michael—and all of us so called— is the far greater, spiritual task yet at hand.

As for the future, we are just beginning. It remains to be seen whether all this might be only part of a wave that appears visible on history's shore and disappears back into the ocean, or whether the Lord is, indeed, bringing from his depths a word, a message for his people, a renewal of Spirit, a call in the face of world decay, a work of his own that will be set upon rock and will not go down again into sand.

And, as always, he has entrusted his shining promises to the care of merest clay.

Time will tell.

Sister Cheri White
Directress, Women's Community
Little Portion Franciscan Hermitage